Kari Daniels, M.A., CCC-SLP & Connie Schaper

About Authors

Kari Daniels M.A., CCC-SLP, received her Bachelor of Science degree in communication disorders from the University of Nebraska-Kearney. She received her Master of Arts from University of South Dakota. She holds a Certificate of Clinical Competence from the American Speech/Language/Hearing Association. She has several years of experience working with children and adults with communication impairments. At present, she is employed by the Oliver/Mercer Special Education Unit as a Speech Language Pathologist.

Connie Schaper received her Bachelor of Science degree in Special and Elementary Education from the University of North Dakota. Mrs. Schaper has several years of experience teaching children with special needs. At present, she is employed by the Oliver/Mercer Special Education Unit and works as a Special Educator in the Beulah Public Schools.

Mayer-Johnson, Inc.
P.O. Box 1579
Solana Beach, CA 92075-7579
U.S.A.

Phone (858) 550-0084
Fax (858) 550-0449
e-mail mayerj@mayer-johnson.com

Second Printing, April 2000

Printed in the U.S.A.

ISBN 1-884135-37-4

Dedicated

To our families, friends and the students at Beulah Elementary who love to go "Out and About."

Table Of Contents

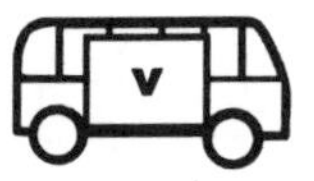

Post Office 65

Library 81

Bowling Alley 97

Hotel 113

Dr. Office/Hospital 129

Police/Fire Department 143

Introduction
School Bus

Introduction

Rationale

Going Out and About is based on the belief that children learn best by doing. The fact that these activities take place in the community reduces the need to focus on generalizing the targeted skills. Each chapter focuses on a specific establishment found in most communities regardless of their population. Throughout this book, you will find activities relating to the following:

- ♦ Recreation
- ♦ Health
- ♦ Safety
- ♦ Independent Living

Several visits to each establishment will be required in order for students to master skills at each level. Ideally, students should be visiting the same establishment on a weekly basis with reinforcement of the targeted skills occurring in the classroom between visits. For this reason, related activities, toys, worksheets, and software options have been included in this program.

Incorporating Into the IEP

This program is meant to be used as an integral part of a child's education; as such, specific goals and objectives relating to its use should be incorporated into a student's IEP. Charting forms which allow for easy monitoring of a student's progress have been included in each chapter. These charts will provide parents and administrators with tangible evidence of a student's progress when you meet with them throughout the year. Do not forget to address special transportation requirements in your student's IEP.

Sample Goal: Johnny will demonstrate knowledge of and access goods and services within the community at his ability level.

Sample Objective: Johnny will use his communication board to complete Level 1 activities with 90-100% accuracy.

NOTE: A student should demonstrate mastery of several Level I boards and activities before progressing to Level II communication boards.

Parent Involvement

Parent involvement is a key aspect of this program. Parents need to be made aware of the benefits of this program before you begin. We recommend that you have a conference with parents to go over the skills you plan to work on with their child. Show them the communication boards and the charting forms. Parents will be much more likely to sign the multiple permission slips you will be sending home if they are aware of the potential benefits to their child. Once their child has mastered the skills at a particular level, be sure to provide the parent with a copy of the communication board and the carrier phrases you used with their child so that parents may continue to work on these skills.

Contacting a Business

Common courtesy dictates the need to contact each business before you take your class on each trip. Suggested steps:

- This is best done in person. If that is not possible, then attempt to contact the business by phone.
- Ask to speak to the manager. Tell him/her your job title and what you plan to do and what you hope to accomplish.
- Ask them what their busiest time of day is and try to avoid that time. You will be able to accomplish more if the establishment is not too busy. The staff will also have more time to devote to you and your students if you arrive at off-peak times.

We have found most establishments to be very supportive of our efforts. If you find a manager to be very resistant to this program, try to find another comparable business and approach them.

Key Point: Be clear about what you plan to do at their establishment. Assure them that the students will be supervised at all times and remember that you are ultimately responsible for the behavior of your students.

Using Activity Pages and Supplemental Worksheets

The activity pages and worksheets are designed to reinforce some of the skills you will be practicing during your community trips. Your students can complete these pages either before you go or after you return. These pages incorporate fine motor skills such as coloring and cutting. Many children may require assistance in completing these pages.

TIP: Activity Page Lamination Steps:

- After coloring, laminate page 1 of the cut-and-paste activity page to a sturdy piece of poster board.
- After coloring, laminate page 2 pieces and cut them out.
- Place reusable adhesive (such as Fun-Tak®) on the back of the cutout pictures to allow them to adhere to page 1.

This is particularly useful for children who require the use of slant boards to complete various activities. The lamination allows students to practice these pages again and again. Don't forget to send them home to allow parents to practice these skills with their children!

The worksheets should be used in the classroom after you have been out in the community. Students can indicate their answers in a variety of ways. Some students may be able to read the worksheet and circle the appropriate answers independently. Other students may need special assistance in these areas. Be sure that adaptive equipment such as pointers and switches are made available for children who need it.

Using the Communication Boards

The communication boards are the main focus of this program. They are appropriate for classroom and home use, so be sure to provide parents with a copy of the communication boards once your student has achieved success at a particular level and at a particular establishment. You may wish to color-code portions of the communication boards to enable your students to quickly locate items on their board.

Suggested Color Codes:
Money = green
Social Words = orange
Places = blue
Nouns = yellow

TIP: Laminating these communication boards and placing them on a clip board will make them more durable and easier for some students to use. Be sure to include the supplemental boards which include specific items where available. You may want to use these boards to create customized boards for a particular student.

The Classroom Environment

A list of related toys and software has been included in each chapter. Be sure to have as many of these items as possible available in the classroom to help reinforce the skills you are targeting. If several students are working on skills at different establishments, you may want to set up learning centers in your classroom that contain the specific items relating to each student and their targeted skills.

Examples of Students at Levels I, II, and III

Level I Student

A level I student is a student who is just beginning to use an alternative means of communication. The focus of level I activities is centered around establishing a consistent yes/no response. The pictures at this level are much larger which will enable students with fine motor limitations to be more successful. These activities are appropriate for students demonstrating moderate to severe cognitive impairments or delays.

Level II Student

A level II student has an established and consistent yes/no response and is ready for the introduction of more concepts including number skills. The activities at this level are centered around labeling and establishing one-to-one correspondence. Students will begin to use their communication boards to interact more independently with others. Social skills such as the use of "please" and "thank you" are introduced at this level. These activities are appropriate for students demonstrating mild to moderate cognitive impairments or delays.

Level III Student

A level III student may possess normal cognitive abilities or a mild impairment or delay. This student is capable of interacting independently with others in his/her environment. These communication boards are designed to encourage this by providing opportunities for the student to practice the skills necessary for independent living. Money skills and management are important skills to be mastered at this level.

Establishing a Transition Work Site

1. Call the business and set up a conference time with the manager of the establishment.
2. Discuss your student's abilities as well as the specific tasks they would be able to perform.
3. Clearly define supervision requirements; i.e., Will you directly supervise your student? Will your student be shadowing an employee independently?
4. Establish a work schedule.
5. Make transportation arrangements.
6. Set up a monitoring schedule to communicate with the management as well as your student's co-workers to check on progress and work habits.
7. Check with your school's administration to determine if transition placements will count towards graduation requirements.

Key Point: Continuous communication is the key to a successful experience.

Permission Slip

Dear Parents,

Our class is planning a field trip to______________________on___________.
During our trip we plan to work on appropriate community social skills, fine motor skills, as well as vocabulary and language skills. We think that some of the best learning takes place in the "real world." The planned student/adult ratio is____to____.
We hope you will allow your child to accompany us on our trip. We feel it will be a safe, fun, and educational experience. If you have any questions or concerns, please feel free to contact me at _______________.

Sincerely,

✂ -

I (we) the parents or guardians of ____________________, give our permission to
(Child's Name)
participate in a field trip to _________________________on__________________.
I (we) also do hereby give and grant onto any medical doctor or hospital our consent and authorization to render such aid, treatment, or care to said participant as, in the judgment of said doctor or hospital, may be required on an emergency basis, in the event said participant should be injured or stricken ill while participating in this outing.

Parent Signature______________________________ Date _______________

Daytime Phone # ______________________

Resources

Resources For Related Toys

Constructive Playthings
1227 East 119th Street
Grandview, MO 64030
800.832.0572

Discovery Toys
2530 Arnold Drive
Martinez, CA 94553
800.426.4777

Fisher Price Inc.
East Aurora, NY 14052
800.432.5437

Kaplan
P.O. Box 609
1310 Lewisville-Clemmons Road
Lewisville, NC 27023
800.334.2014

Lakeshore Learning Materials
2695 E. Dominguez Street
P.O. Box 6261
Carson, CA 90749
800.421.5354

Lilly's Kids
Lillian Vernon Corporation
Virginia Beach, VA 23479
800.285.5555

Little Tikes Co.
Hudson, OH 44236

National Parent Network on Disabilities
1600 Prince Street, #115
Alexandria, VA 22314
703.684.6763

Toys R Us
P.O. Box 8501
Nevada, IA 50201

Summit Learning
P.O. Box 493
Ft. Collins, CO 80522
800.777.8817

Re-Print Corporation
P.O. Box 830677
Birmingham, AL 35283
800.248.9171

Augmentative Communication & Adaptive Equipment Resources

Ablenet, Inc.
1081 Tenth Avenue S.E.
Minneapolis, MN 55414
619.322.0956

Communication Aids for Children and Adults
Crestwood Company
6625 N. Sidney Place
Milwaukee, WI 53209
414.352.5678

Edmark
P.O. Box 97021
Redmond, WA 98073
800.362.2890

Innocomp
26210 Emery Road Suite 302
Warrensville Heights, OH 44128

IntelliTools, Inc.
55 Leveroni Court
Novato, CA 94949
800.899.6687

Mayer-Johnson, Inc.
P.O. Box 1579
Solana Beach, CA 92075
858.550.0084

Prentke Romich Company
1022 Heyl Road
Wooster, OH 44691
800.262.1984

Sentient Systems, Inc.
2100 Wharton St.
Pittsburgh, PA 15203
800.344.1778

TASH
Unit 1-91 Station Street
Ajax, Ontario, Canada L1S 3H2
800.463.5685

Technology for Education
2300 Lexington Ave. S. Suite, 202
St. Paul, MN 55120
800.370.0047

Zygo Industries, Inc.
P.O. Box 1008
Portland, OR 97207
800.234.6006

Augmentative Communication & Adaptive Equipment Resources

Ablenet, Inc.
1081 Tenth Avenue S.E.
Minneapolis, MN 55414
619.322.0956

Communication Aids for Children and Adults
Crestwood Company
6625 N. Sidney Place
Milwaukee, WI 53209
414.352.5678

Edmark
P.O. Box 97021
Redmond, WA 98073
800.362.2890

Innocomp
26210 Emery Road Suite 302
Warrensville Heights, OH 44128

IntelliTools, Inc.
55 Leveroni Court
Novato, CA 94949
800.899.6687

Mayer-Johnson Co.
P.O. Box 1579
Solana Beach, CA 92075
619.550.0084

Prentke Romich Company
1022 Heyl Road
Wooster, OH 44691
800.262.1984

Sentient Systems, Inc.
2100 Wharton St.
Pittsburgh, PA 15203
800.344.1778

TASH
Unit 1-91 Station Street
Ajax, Ontario, Canada L1S 3H2
800.463.5685

Technology for Education
2300 Lexington Ave. S. Suite, 202
St. Paul, MN 55120
800.370.0047

Zygo Industries, Inc.
P.O. Box 1008
Portland, OR 97207
800.234.6006

Grocery Store
Dept. Store
Restaurant
Gas Station
Post Offic
Library
Bowling Alley
Hotel
Hospital
Police/Fire
hool Bus

Grocery Store

Getting Ready To Go

1. First tell your class where you are going on your trip and practice using your communication boards.
2. Discuss the behavior you expect (you may need to model appropriate behavior and do some role playing).
3. Plan your list with the class.
4. Clip coupons if they are available.
5. Designate responsibilities (see Job List, page 11).
6. Preprogram switches/augmentative communication devices to reflect the field trip you are taking.
7. Practice money skills.
8. Check to make sure all permission slips have been signed.
9. Bring supplemental fruit and vegetable communication board.
10. Grab the communication boards and lets go!!!

Vocabulary List

color words, smooth, bumpy, big, little
wet, dry, cold, up, down
middle, top, bottom, shelf, bag
cart, register, price, clerk, open
close, push, pull

Language Skills

categorizing
sentence structure
turn-taking skills
labeling
switch use
identifying attributes
pragmatic skills

Fine Motor Skills

opening/closing vehicle door
handling items
carrying items
pushing/pulling door
twisting produce fasteners
bagging groceries
maneuvering cart
handling money
cutting

Picture Vocabulary Words

Directions: Use the picture vocabulary words to review words and symbols that are new to your students.

Grocery Store Activities

Level I

1. Show your students different fruits and vegetables. Ask them, *"Is a banana a fruit or a vegetable?"*
2. Have your students indicate yes/no to the following questions:
   "Do we eat this?" (Show them edible and inedible items.)
   "Can we eat food in the store?" (Discuss appropriate behavior.)
   "Is broccoli orange?" (Discuss various colors found in vegetables.)

Level II

1. Have your students identify the texture of different fruits and vegetables. *"How does the apple feel? The apple feels ___________. How does the broccoli feel? The broccoli feels ___________."*
2. Have your students practice number concepts 0-5. *"How many oranges am I holding? How many tomatoes do we need?"*
3. Have your students engage in conversations relating to their likes/dislikes regarding different foods. *"Do you like to eat lemons?"*
4. Have your students ask a clerk for help.

   Suggested sequence:
   "I need help."
   "3." (Insert the number of items desired.)
   "Fruit." (Insert the name of the fruit.)
   "Thank you."

Level III

1. Have your students tell you where you plan to go and what you will be looking for there. *"Where are we going today? What will we be looking for?"*
2. Have your students estimate how many items it will take to make a pound. *"How many pears will it take to make a pound?"*
3. Have your students practice manners and independence by having them ask a store clerk for help.

   Suggested sequence:
   "I need help. Please."
   "Vegetables." (Your students can use the "yes" or "no" to help the clerk find the correct items.)
4. Have your students engage in conversations relating to their likes/dislikes and foods they have and have not tasted before. *"I like that. I don't like that. Have you tasted cauliflower before?"*
5. Have your students ask a clerk to help them find an item in the store.

   Suggested sequence:
   "I need help. Frozen/canned vegetables. Please."

Grocery Store — Level I
Communication Board

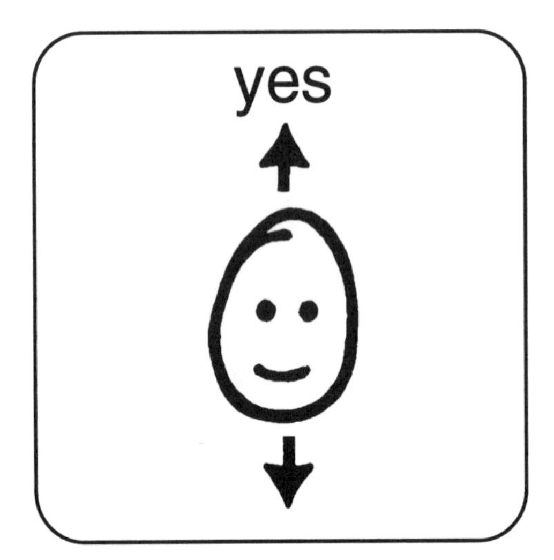

Grocery Store — Level II
Communication Board

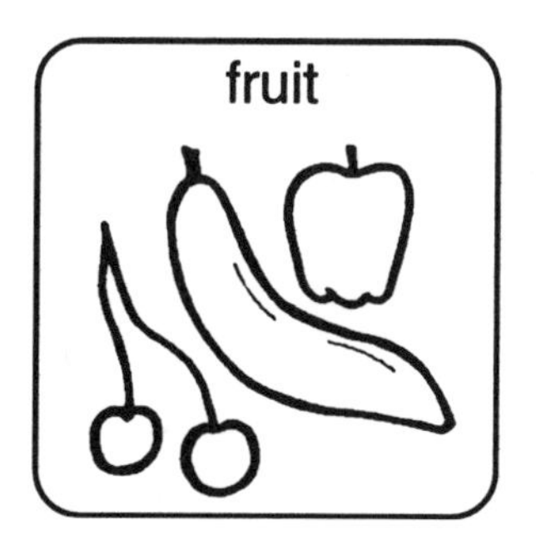

2 3 4 5

Grocery Store — Level III
Communication Board

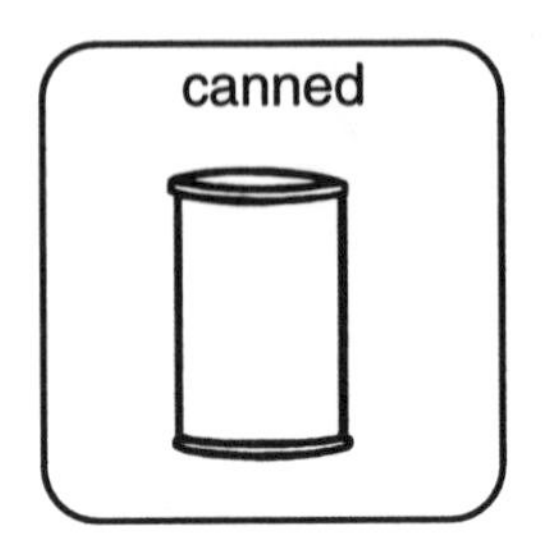

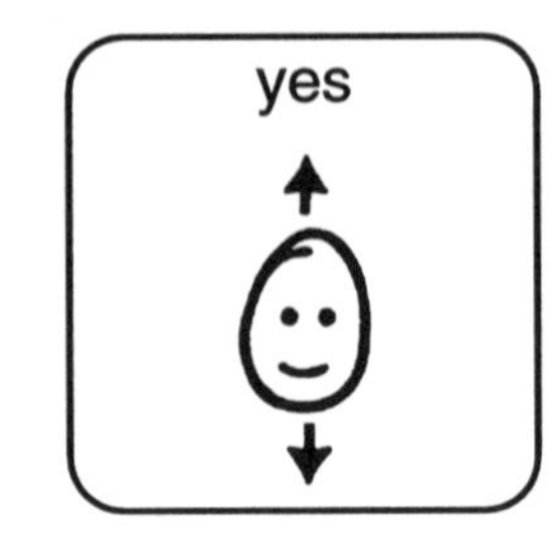

0	1	2	3	4	5	6	7	8	9

Grocery Store
Follow-up Activities

Fine Motor & Follow-up Activities

Have a taste test of the items that you purchased and make a category poster by their taste; e.g. "sour" "sweet" etc.

Cut up fruits and vegetables.
Dip them in paint to create stamp art.

Use the groceries purchased to make your recipe.

Use sales ads from grocery store to practice addition.

Use play foods or empty cartons/ containers to set up and organize a store.

Use play cash register to role-play cashier.

Role-play bag boy—discuss what foods go on the bottom.

Practice opening produce bags. (A real fine-motor challenge sometimes!)

Talk about and practice the appropriate way to handle the produce.
"We have to be gentle with the tomatoes.
We can lightly squeeze the pears.
We cannot put the food in our mouths."

Practice using the fasteners to close the bag.

Transition Activities for Older Students

- Practice using a checkbook.
- Develop a resume.
- Practice interviewing skills by role playing.
- Bag and/or carry out groceries.
- Stock and dust shelves.
- Sweep the floors.
- Discard cardboard boxes.

All of the work activities will initially require supervision. If your student is high functioning, this may eventually turn into an independent work situation. Refer to introduction regarding developing work sites, page I-7.

Grocery Store Worksheet

Name:______________________________ Date:______________

1. Which item is a fruit?

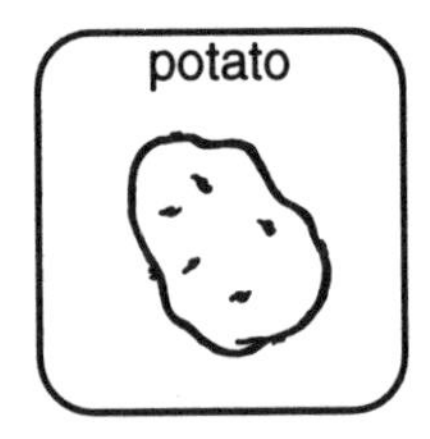

2. Which item is a vegetable?

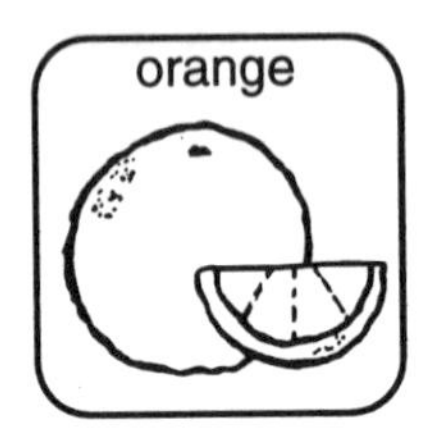

3. Which vegetable is orange?

4. Which fruit is sour?

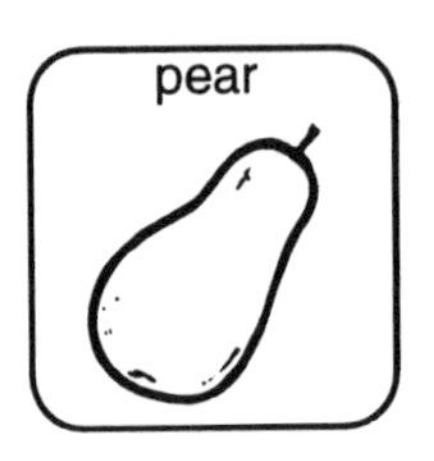

5. Which vegetable has seeds inside?

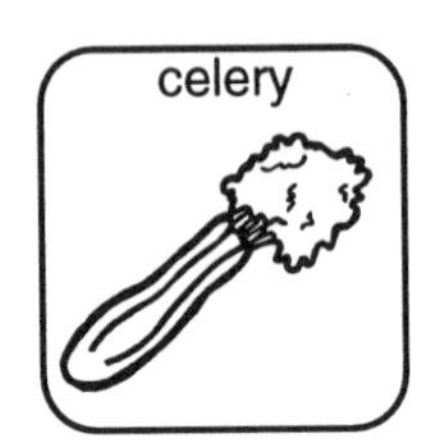

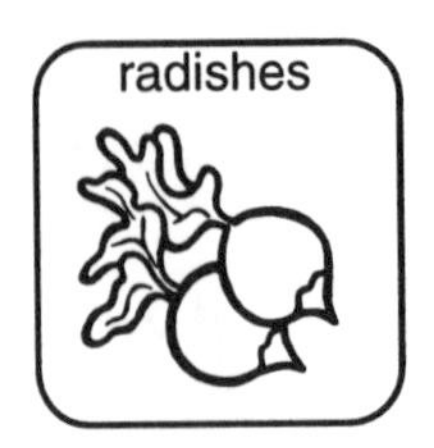

Grocery Store
Job List

Opening Doors ______________________

____

Pushing Cart ______________________

____

Selecting Items ______________________

____

Removing Items From Cart ______________________

____

Handling Money ______________________

____

Bagging Groceries ______________________

____

Switches Programmed For ______________________

____

Grocery Store Follow-up Activity

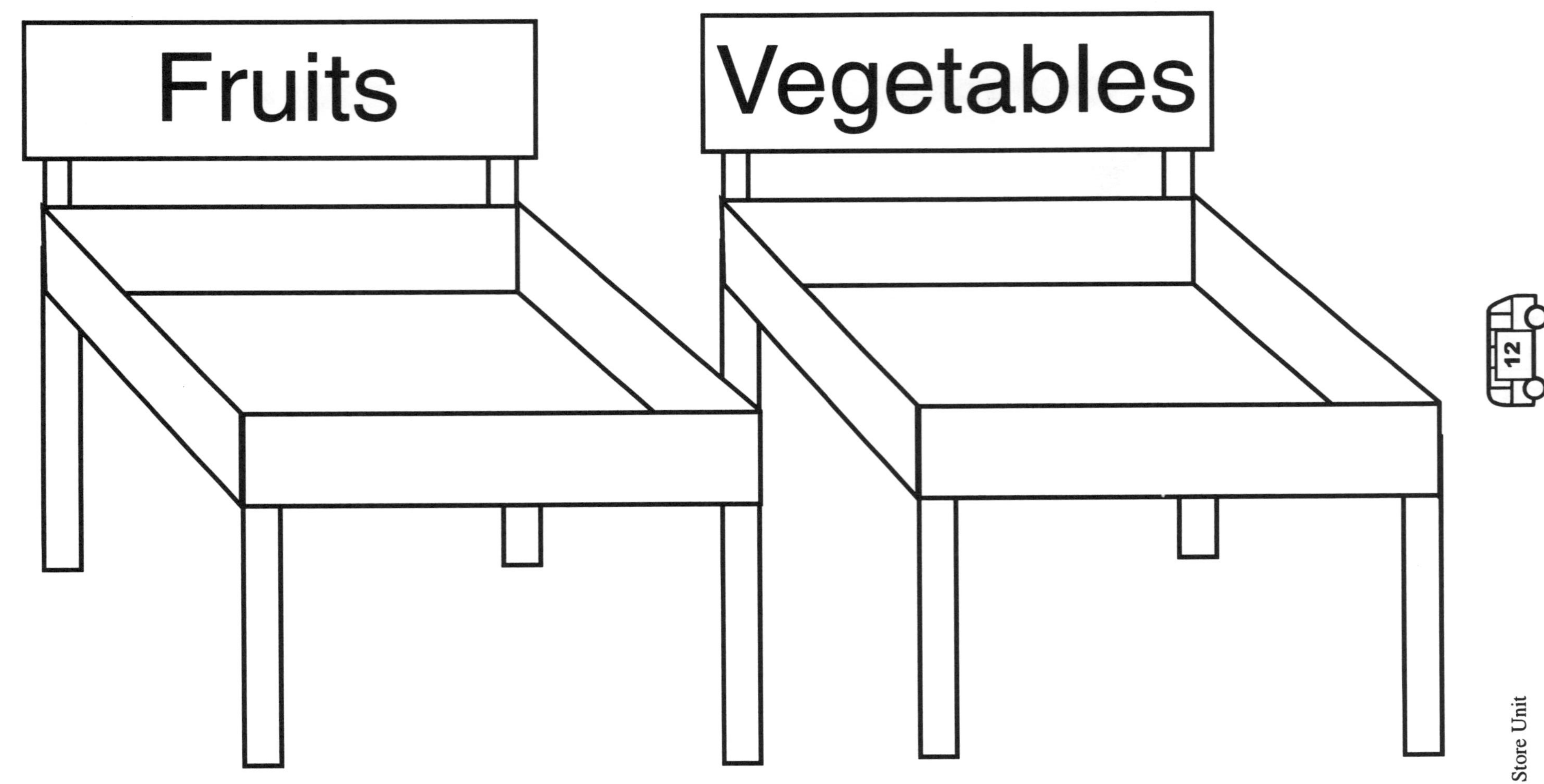

Grocery Store Follow-up Activity Cutouts

Directions: The following items are to be used with the Grocery Store Follow-up Activity, page 12. Duplicate both pages. Color, cut out, and laminate items on this page. Attach a reusable adhesive (such as Fun-Tak®) to the back of each item. In addition, color, and laminate the Grocery Store Follow-up Activity page. As you say the name of the item, have the student place it in the correct vegetable or fruit bin.

Grocery Store Charting Form

Name ____________________

DATE				
Big				
Little				
Up				
Down				
Middle				
Top				
Bottom				
Bag				
Cart				
Register				
Price				
Clerk				
Smooth				
Bumpy				
Wet				
Dry				
Cold				
Shelf				
Open				
Close				
Push				
Pull				
Yes				
No				
Please				
Thank you				

FINE MOTOR				
Opening Door				
Closing Door				
Cutting				
Coloring				
Pushing Cart				
Handling Items				
Twist Ties				
Handling Money				
Carrying Items				
Bagging Items				

VP = Verbal Prompt   PP = Physical Prompt   HH = Hand Over Hand   + = Independent   - = Incapable

Notes:

Grocery Store
Related Materials

Books

Tops & Bottoms adapted by Janet Stevens. NY:Scholastic, 1995.
Growing Vegetable Soup by Lois Ehlert. NY:Scholastic, 1987.
Eating Fractions by Bruce McMillan. NY:Scholastic Inc., 1991.
Eating the Alphabet by Lois Ehlert. NY:Trumpet Club, 1989.
Just Shopping with Mom by Mercer Mayer. NY:Western, 1989.
Something Good by Robert Munsch. Ontario:Firefly Books, 1990.
Hare & Bear Go Shopping by Julie E. Frankel. MO:Milliken, 1990.
The Berenstain Bears at the Super-Duper Market by Stan & Jan Berenstain. NY:Random House, Inc., 1991.

Related Software

Community Exploration available through Edmark
TouchMoney by Edmark
Grocery Words by Edmark
Comparison Kitchens available through Cambridge Development Laboratory
Fun Around Town available through SoftWareHouse
Bake and Taste available through Edmark
Shopping Dictionary available through Edmark
Shopping Smart Software available through Academic Communication Associates

Related Toys

Shopping cart
Play food
Cash register
Play money
Shopping bags
Supermarket Uniset

Grocery Store Supplemental Board
Fruits and Vegetables

apple

banana

cherries

grapefruit

grapes

lemon

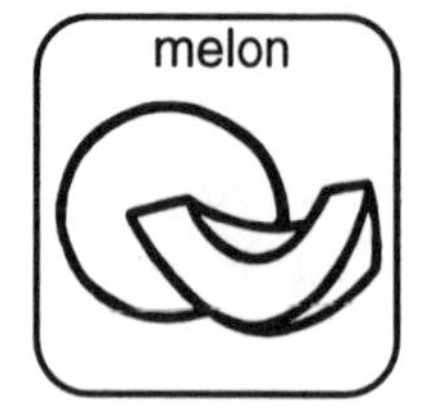
melon

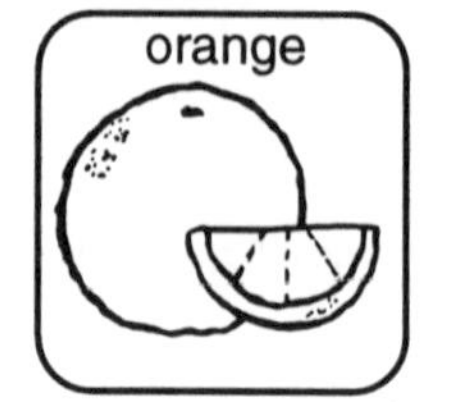
orange

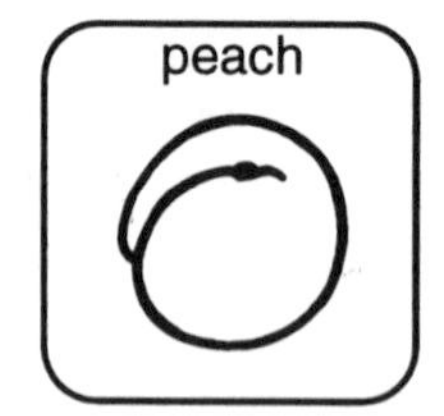
peach

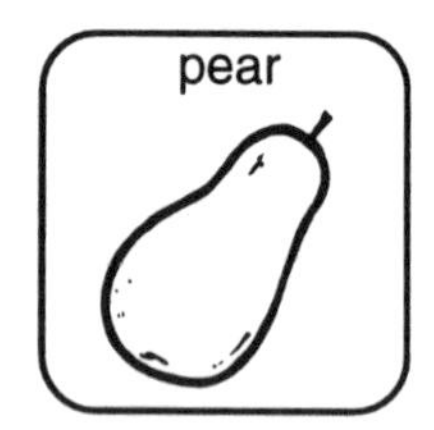
pear

pineapple

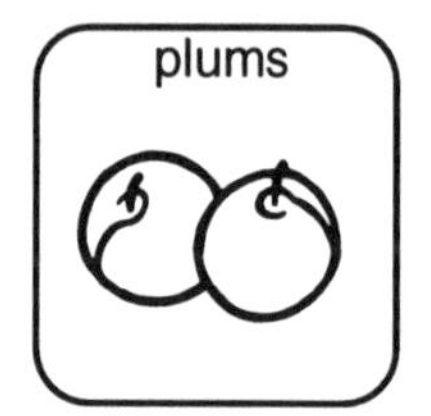
plums

strawberry

watermelon

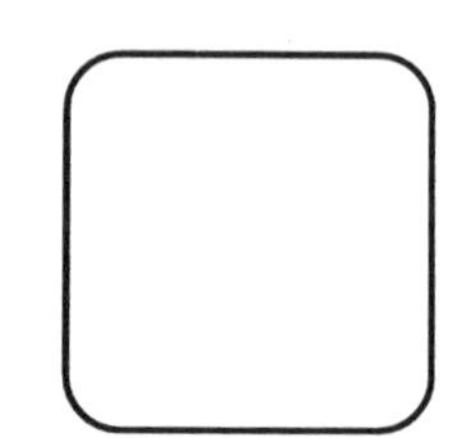

asparagus

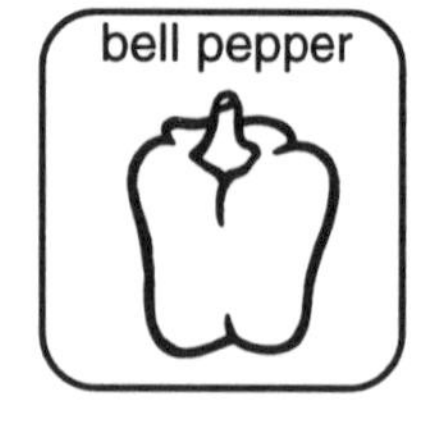
bell pepper

broccoli

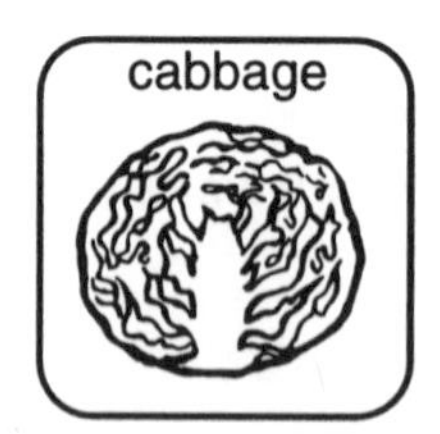
cabbage

carrot

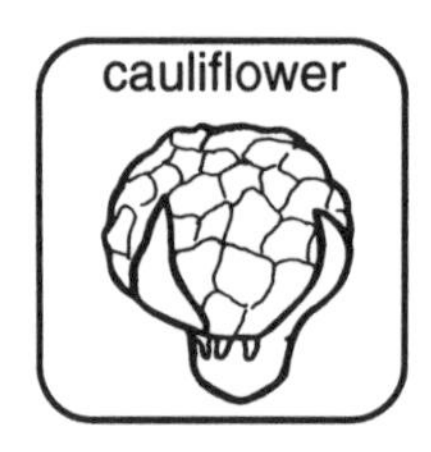
cauliflower

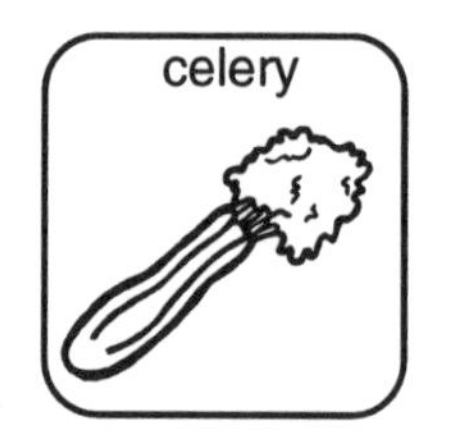
celery

corn

cucumber

lettuce

mushrooms

onions

peas

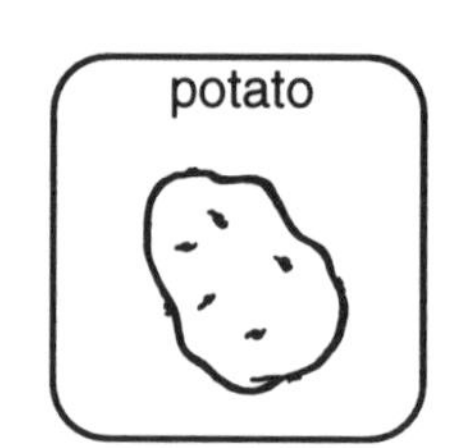
potato

tomato

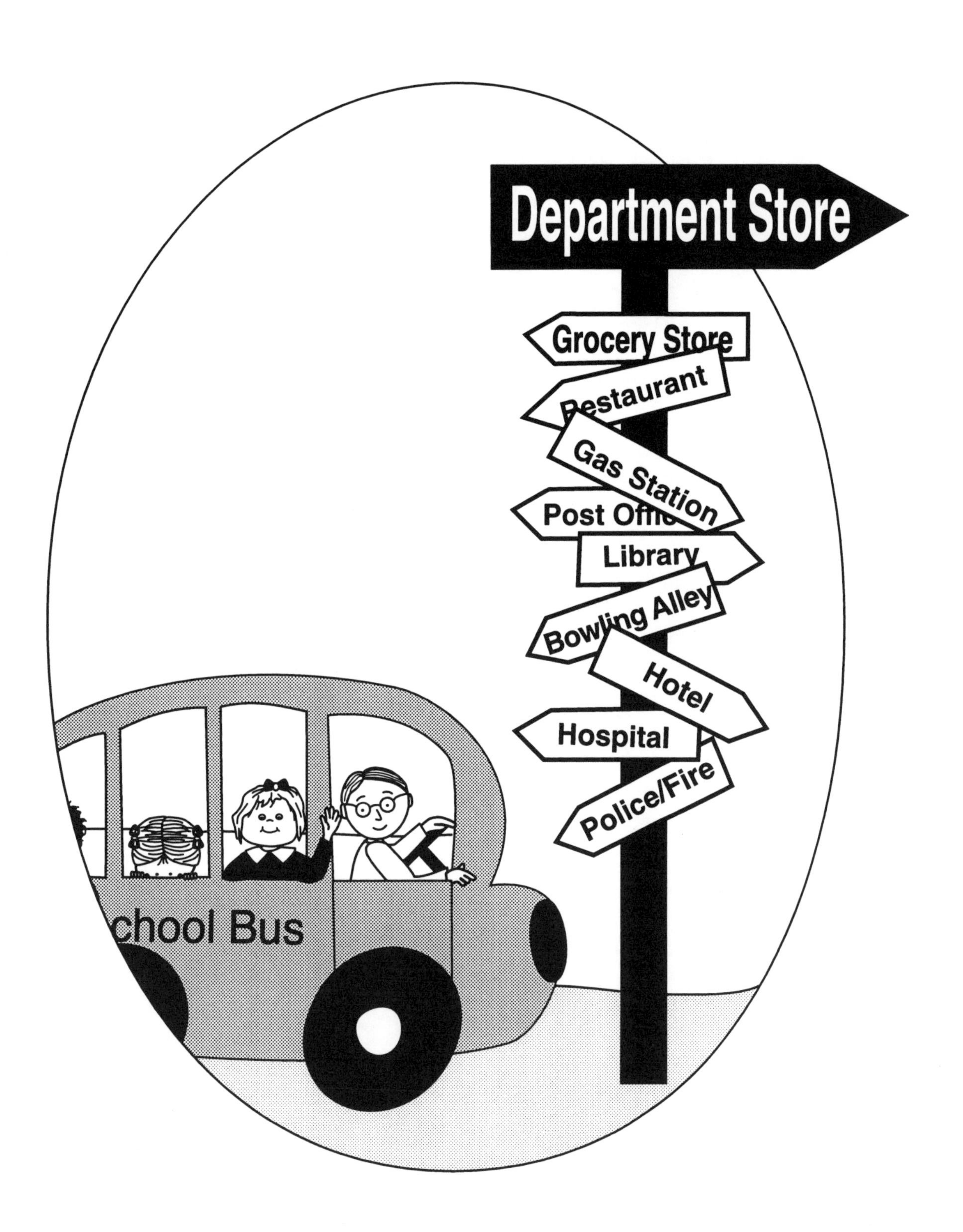

Department Store
Grocery Store
Restaurant
Gas Station
Post Offi
Library
Bowling Alley
Hotel
Hospital
Police/Fire
chool Bus

Department Store 

Getting Ready To Go

1. First tell you class where you are going on your trip and practice using your communication boards.
2. Discuss the behavior you expect (you may need to model appropriate behavior and do some role playing).
3. Determine students' clothing sizes.
4. Designate responsibilities (see Job List, page 27).
5. Preprogram switches/augmentative communication devices to reflect the field trip you are taking.
6. Practice money skills.
7. Check to make sure all permission slips have been signed.
8. Grab the communication boards and let's go!!!

Vocabulary List

color words	numbers	big	little	up
down	middle	top	bottom	bag
cart	register	price	clerk	shirt
pants	open	close	push	pull
yes	no	please	thank you	

Language Skills

categorizing	labeling	identifying attributes
sentence structure	switch use	pragmatic skills

Fine Motor Skills

opening/closing doors	maneuvering cart	folding
opening/closing fasteners	hanging clothing on hangers	sorting
handling money	carrying items	cutting
coloring		

Picture Vocabulary Words

Directions: Use the picture vocabulary words to review words and symbols that are new to your students.

Department Store
Activities

Level I

1. Show your students the different articles of clothing found in the store. Have them use their communication boards to categorize these items. *"Is this a shirt or a pair of pants?"*
2. Discuss the clothes your students are wearing. Touch an article of their clothing and ask them what it is. *"What is this?"*
3. Have your students indicate yes/no to the following questions:
   "Would this fit you?" (Use an item that is too big or too small.)
   "Would you wear this on your head?" (Show him/her pants.)
   "Is this shirt blue?" (Find items of all colors and discuss them.)

Level II

1. Have your students label various items found in the store. Ask them, *"What is this?"*
2. Show your students different articles of clothing. Have your student indicate whether this item would be too big or too small for them. *"Would this be too big or too small for you?"*
3. Have your students use their communication boards to indicate yes or no to the following questions:
   "Is this for a boy?" (Hold up a tie, etc.)
   "Is this for a girl?" (Hold up a dress, etc.)
   "Would this fit me?"
4. Have your students practice number concepts 0-5. *"How many pockets do these pants have? How many buttons are on this shirt? How many shoes come in a pair?"*
5. Have your students ask a clerk for help.
   Suggested sequence:
   "I need help. Shirt. Too small. Thank you."

Level III

1. Have your students tell you where you plan to go and what you will find there. *"Where are we going today? What will we find there?"*
2. Have your students estimate the cost of possible items to be purchased. *"How much would this shirt and these pants cost?"*
3. Have your students use their communication board to ask a clerk for help.
   Suggested sequence:
   "I need help. Please. How much is it? Thank you."
4. Show your students different articles of clothing. Have your student indicate whether this item would be too big or too small for them. *"Would this be too big or too small for you?"*
5. Have your students engage in conversations relating to their likes/dislikes regarding different styles of clothing. *"Would you wear a shirt like this?"*
6. Have your students ask where the bathroom is located.
   Suggested sequence:
   "I need help. Please. Bathroom Thank you."

Department Store — Level I
Communication Board

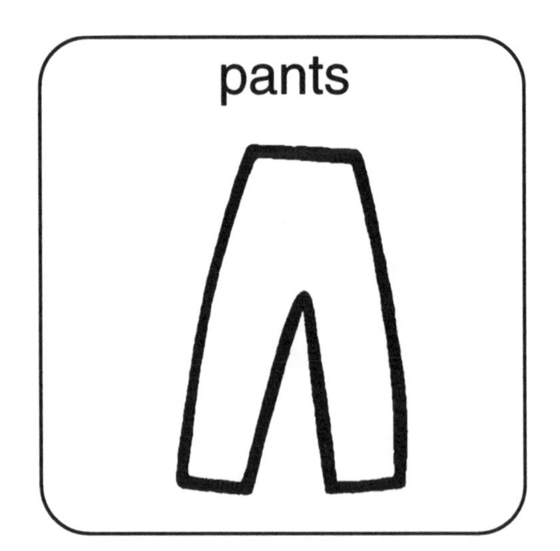

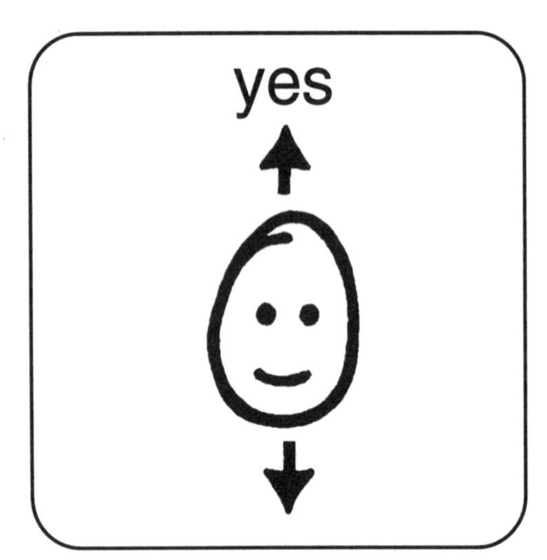

Department Store — Level II
Communication Board

Department Store — Level III
Communication Board

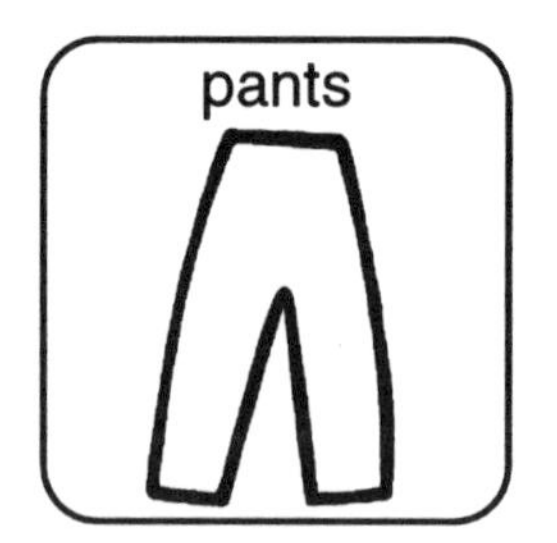

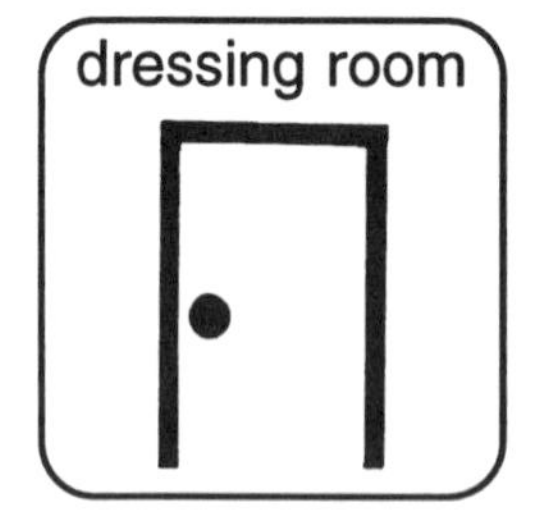

0	1	2	3	4	5	6	7	8	9

Department Store
Follow-up Activities

Fine Motor & Follow-up Activities

 Practice buttoning, snapping, tying shoes, fastening zippers.

 Use material scraps to create paper doll clothing.

 Practice folding clothes and placing them on hangers.

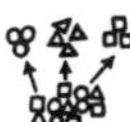 Sort buttons and socks.

 Play dress up.

 Practice using cash register.

Transition Activities for Older Students

- Sweep floors.
- Carry out customer's packages.
- Hang up clothing for displays.
- Stock and dust shelves.
- Develop a resume.
- Practice interviewing skills.
- Practice checkbook management.

All on-site work activities will initially require supervision. If your student is high functioning, this may eventually turn into an independent work situation. Refer to introduction regarding developing work sites, page I-7.

Department Store Worksheet

Name:______________________ Date:____________

1. What would you wear in the summer?

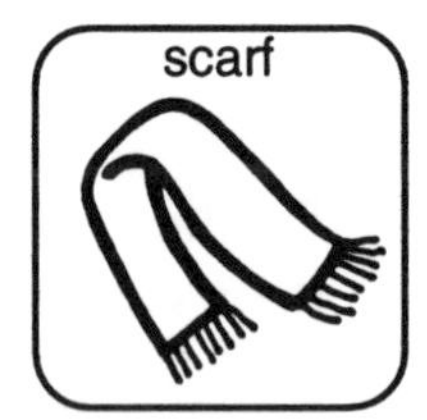

2. What would you wear in the winter?

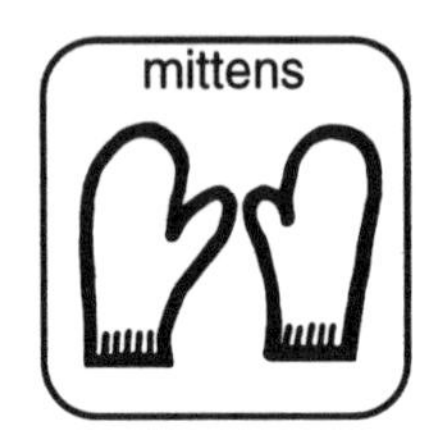

3. What would you wear at bedtime?

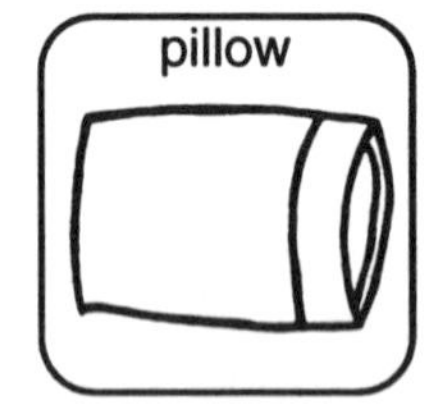

4. What do you wear on your feet?

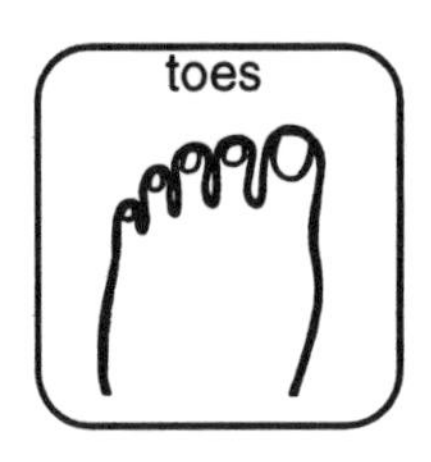

5. What do you wear on your head?

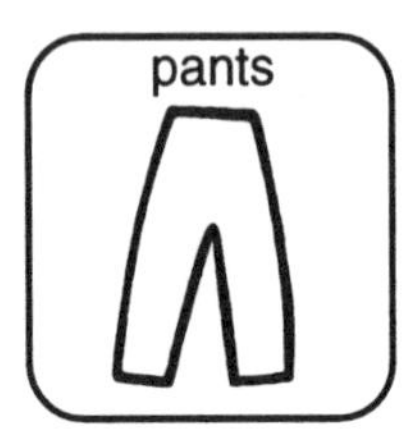

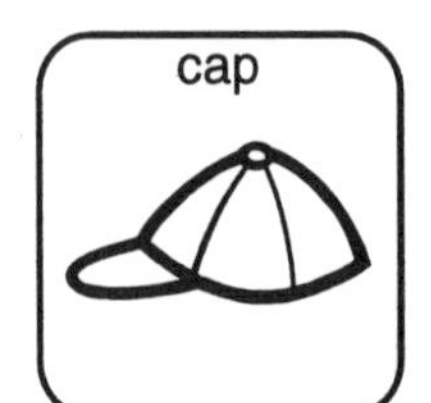

Department Store
Job List

Opening Doors ____________________

____

Pushing Cart ____________________

____

Selecting Items ____________________

____

Removing Items From Cart ____________________

____

Bagging Items ____________________

____

Carrying Items ____________________

____

Switches Programmed For ____________________

____

Department Store Follow-up Activity

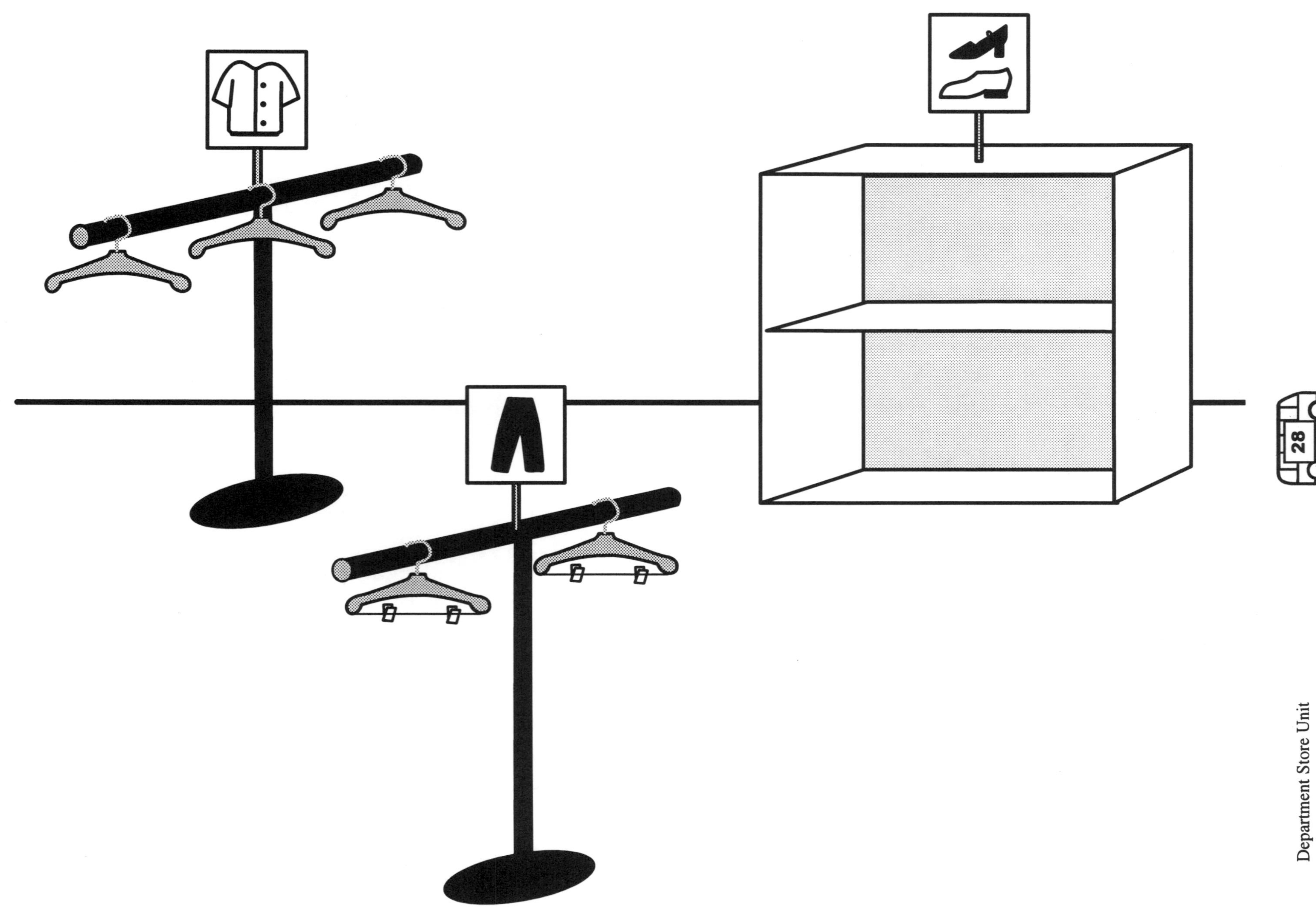

Dept. Store Follow-up Activity Cutouts

Directions: The following items are to be used with the Department Store Follow-up Activity, page 28. Duplicate both pages. Color, cut out, and laminate items on this page. Attach reusable adhesive (such as Fun-tak®) to the back of each item. In addition, color, and laminate the Department Store Follow-up Activity page. As you say the name of the item, have the student place it in the correct location for pants, shirts, and shoes.

Dept. Store Charting Form

Name ____________________

DATE				
Big				
Little				
Up				
Down				
Middle				
Top				
Bottom				
Bag				
Cart				
Register				
Price				
Clerk				
Shirt				
Pants				
Shoes				
Open				
Close				
Push				
Pull				
Yes				
No				
Please				
Thank you				

FINE MOTOR				
Opening Door				
Closing Door				
Cutting				
Coloring				
Pushing Cart				
Snaps				
Buttons				
Zippers				
Hanging Clothes				
Sorting				
Handling Money				
Folding				
Carrying Items				

VP = Verbal Prompt   PP = Physical Prompt   HH = Hand Over Hand   + = Independent   - = Incapable

Notes:

Department Store
Related Materials

Books

On Market Street by Arnold Lobel. NY:Greenwillow Books, 1981.
Max's Dragon Shirt by Rosemary Wells. NY:Dial Books, 1991.
Shoes from Grandpa by Mem Fox. NY:Orchard Books, 1989.
Harry Hates Shopping by Ronda Armitage. NY:Scholastic, 1993.
Ernie Gets Lost by Liza Alexander. WI:Western Publishing Co. Inc., 1985.
The Downtown Day by Linda Strauss Edwards. NY:Random House, 1983.
The Storekeeper by Tracey Campbell Pearson. NY:Dial Books, 1988.

Related Software

Community Exploration available through Edmark
TouchMoney by Edmark
Fun Around Town available through SoftWareHouse
Shopping Smart Software available through Academic Communication Associates

Related Toys

Dress-up clothes
Toy cash register
Play money

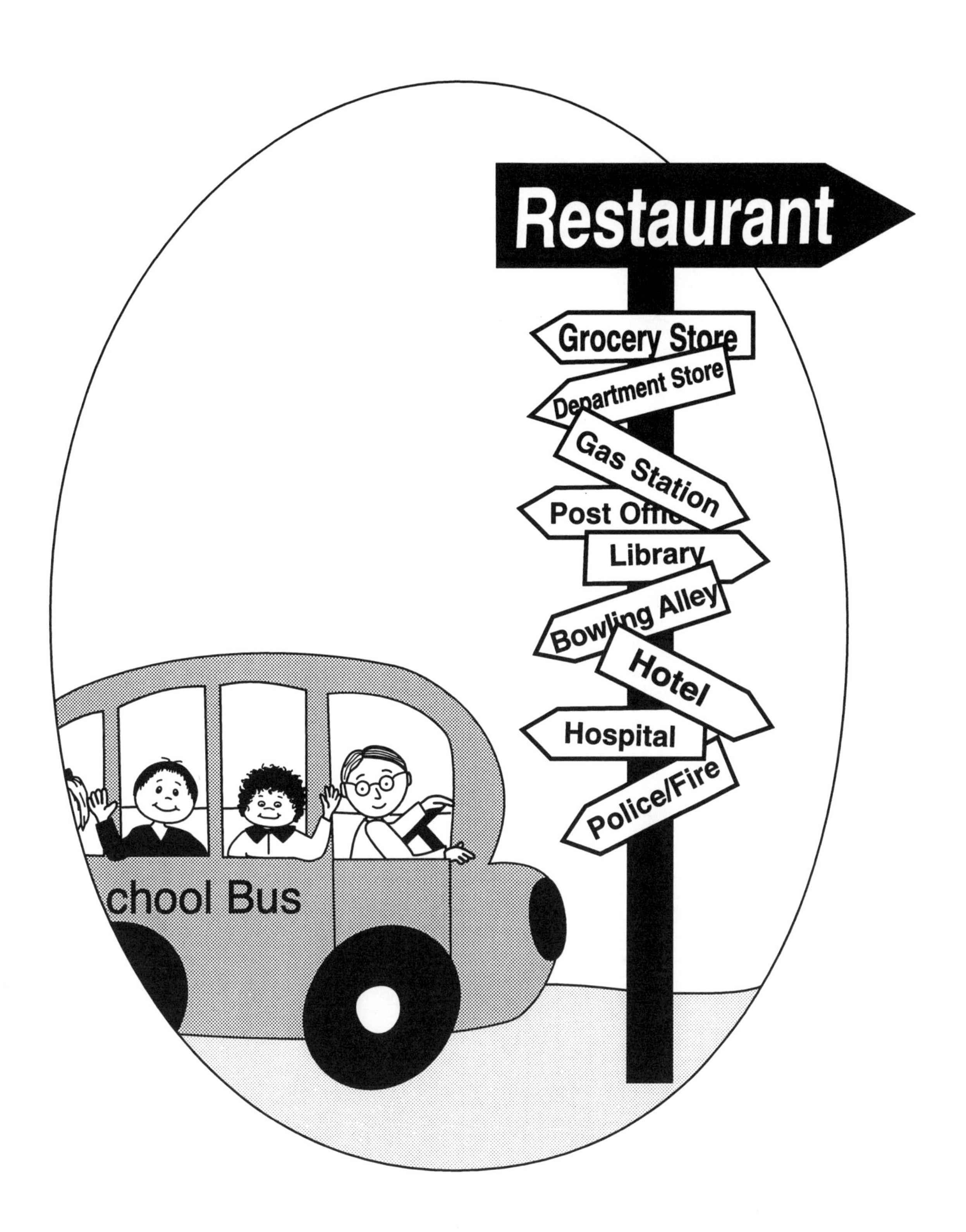
Restaurant
Grocery Store
Department Store
Gas Station
Post Offic
Library
Bowling Alley
Hotel
Hospital
Police/Fire
chool Bus

Restaurant

Getting Ready To Go

1. First tell your class where you are going on your trip and practice using your communication boards.
2. Discuss the behavior you expect (you may need to model appropriate behavior and do some role playing).
3. Plan what you will be ordering.
4. Bring supplemental communication boards with specific food and drink items.
5. Designate responsibilities (see Job List, page 43).
6. Preprogram switches/augmentative communication devices to reflect the field trip you are taking.
7. Practice money skills.
8. Check to make sure all permission slips have been signed.
9. Grab the communication boards and go!!!

Vocabulary List

color words	numbers	small	medium	large
cold	hot	register	price	eat
waiter/waitress	drink	menu	fork	spoon
knife	napkin	straw	open	close
push	pull	yes	no	please
thank you				

Language Skills

categorizing	labeling	identifying attributes
sentence structure	switch use	pragmatic skills

Fine Motor Skills

opening/closing doors	handling money	washing dishes
folding napkins	measuring	using silverware
cutting	coloring	painting
stirring	drinking from straw	

Picture Vocabulary Words

Directions: Use the picture vocabulary words to review words and symbols that are new to your students.

Restaurant
Activities

Level I

1. Show your students an entreé or a picture of an entreé. Ask them, *"What do we do with this?"*
2. Show your students a malt or a soda can. Ask them, *"What do we do with this?"*
3. Have your students indicate yes/no to the following questions:
   "Do we eat this?" (Show them a napkin, chair, french fry, etc.)
   "Do we drink this?" (Show them pop, pudding, silverware, etc.)
   "Do we run in a restaurant?" (Discuss appropriate behavior.)

Level II

1. Show your students the menu or menu board. Ask them, *"What do we look at before we order?"*
2. Show your students a salad bar or buffet table if one is available. Ask them, *"Would this be hot or cold?"*
3. Have your students practice number concepts 0-5 using food items purchased, such as french fries, toast, scoops of ice cream, ice in a glass of ice water. *"How many ____do you see?"*
4. Have your students practice manners and independence by placing a simple order.
   Suggested sequence:
   "I need help. Please. Drink/Item on menu. Thank you."
5. Have your students use their communication board to indicate when they are done. *"Tell me when you are finished."*

Level III

1. Have your students tell you where you plan to go and what you will find there. *"Where are we going today? What will we find there?"*
2. Have your students estimate the cost of possible items purchased. *"How much would a small soda and small order of french fries cost?"*
3. Have your students engage in conversations using their communication board to indicate their likes and dislikes in relation to the menu.
4. Have students respond to yes/no questions from the waiter/waitress using their communication boards. *("Do you want fries with that? Did you want a large drink?")*
5. Have your students use their communication boards to place an order. Students at this level may also be able to order for other students in the group.
   Suggested sequence:
   "I need help. Please. Drink/Item on menu. Thank you."
6. Have your students ask where the bathroom is located.
   Suggested sequence:
   "I need help. Please. Bathroom. Thank you."

Restaurant — Level I
Communication Board

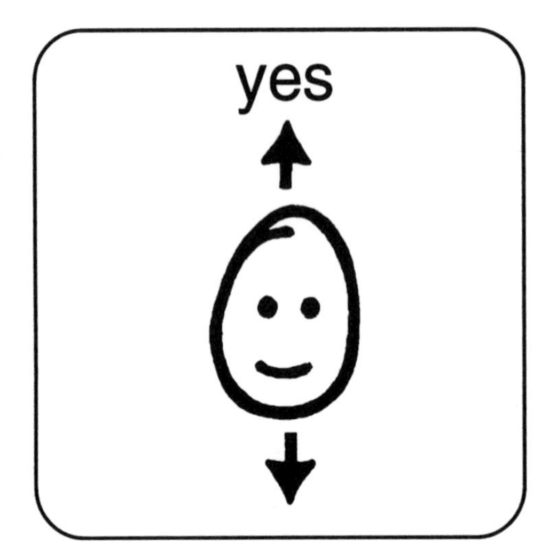

Restaurant — Level II
Communication Board

0

2

3

4

5

Restaurant — Level III
Communication Board

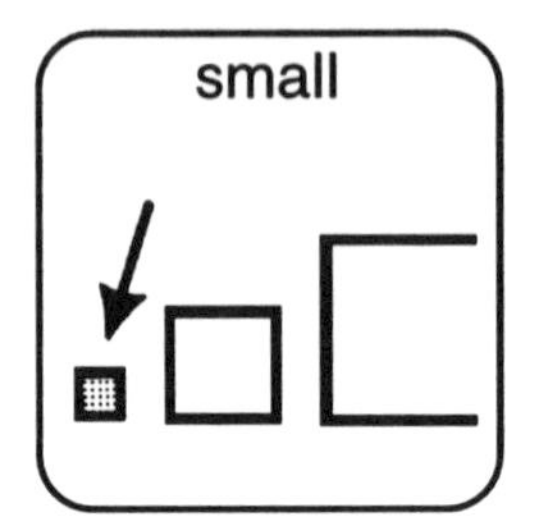

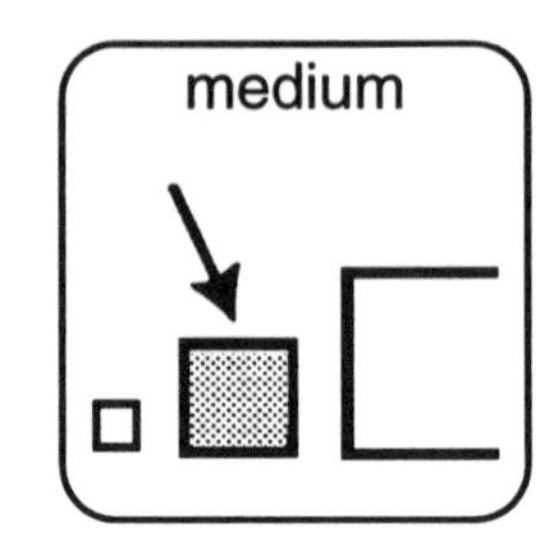

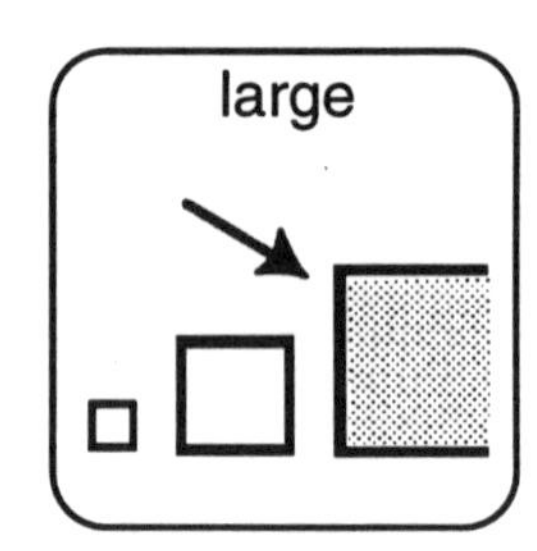

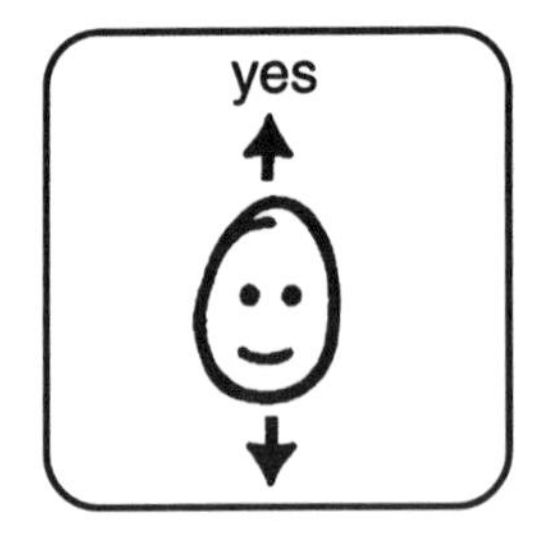

0	1	2	3	4	5	6	7	8	9

Restaurant
Follow-up Activities

Fine Motor & Follow-up Activities

Practice rolling silverware up in napkins.

Role-play (waiter/waitress, bus boy, cook, etc.).

Practice measurement (cup, teaspoon, tablespoon, etc.).

Categorize food by food groups using play food or pictures.

Paint with eating utensils (fork and spoon painting).

Practice washing dishes.

Make simple recipes.

Plan nutritious menu.

Use the menu to practice addition.

Transition Activities for Older Students

- Wash dishes.
- Bus tables.
- Sweep floors.
- Clean bathrooms.
- Roll silverware in napkins.
- Fill condiment trays.
- Develop a resume.
- Practice checkbook management.
- Practice interviewing skills.

All on-site work activities will initially require supervision. If your student is high functioning, this may eventually turn into an independent work situation. Refer to introduction regarding developing worksites, page I-7.

Restaurant Worksheet

Name:______________________________ Date:______________

1. Which item is supposed to be served hot?

2. Which item is supposed to be served cold?

3. Where do you go to eat?

4. What do you look at to order your food?

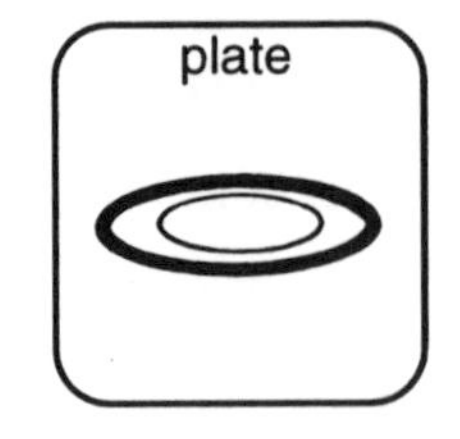

5. Which item is a dessert?

Restaurant
Job List

Opening Doors ______________________

____

Ordering ______________________

____

Handling Money ______________________

____

Carrying Tray ______________________

____

Cleaning Up Table ______________________

____

Getting Condiments/Napkins ______________________

____

Switches Programmed For ______________________

____

Restaurant Follow-up Activity

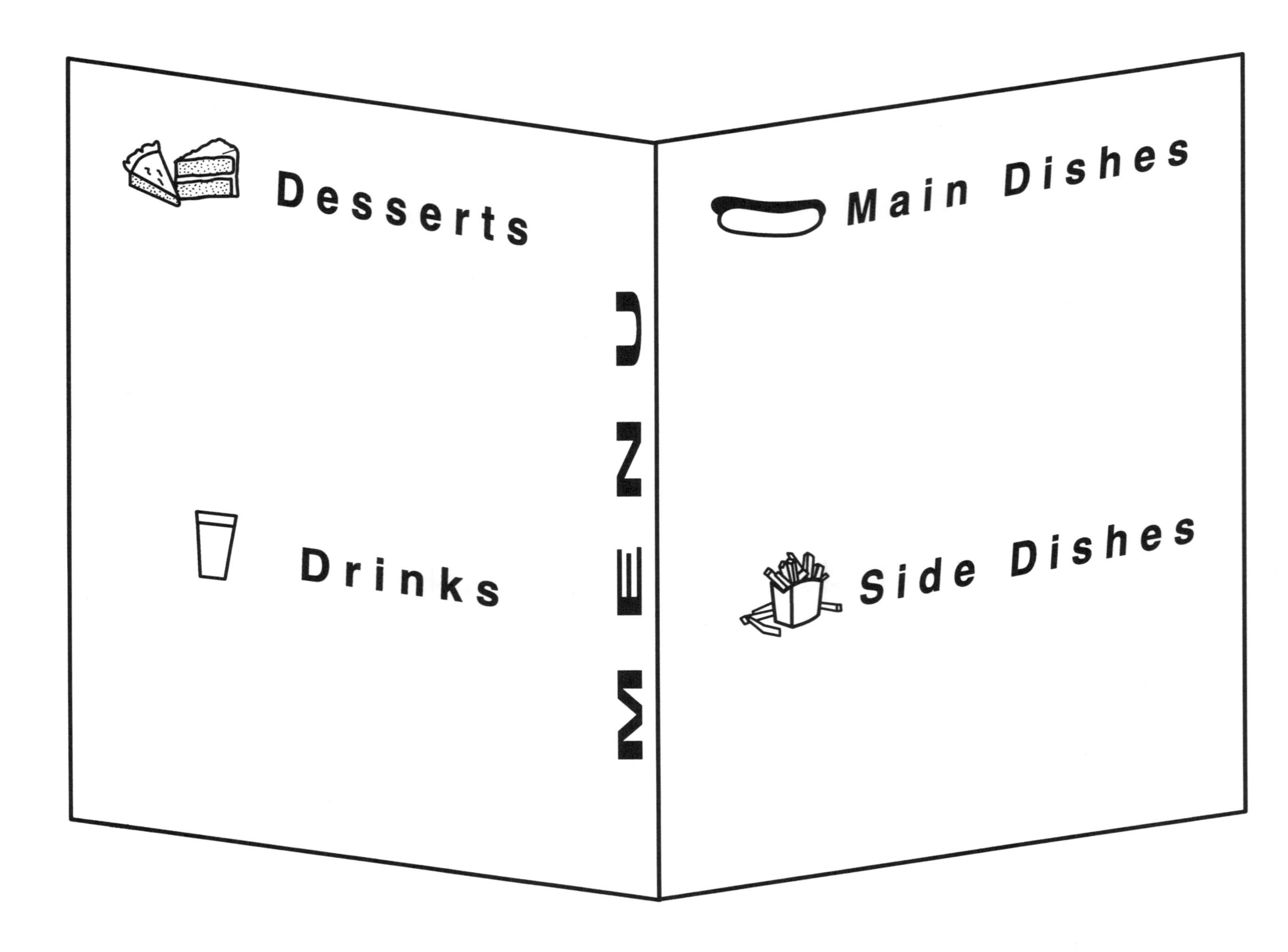

Restaurant Follow-up Activity Cutouts

Directions: The following items are to be used with the Restaurant Follow-up Activity, page 44. Duplicate both pages. Color, cut out, and laminate items on this page. Attach a reusable adhesive (such as Fun-Tak®) to the back of each item. In addition, color and laminate the Restaurant Follow-up Activity Page. As you say the name of the item, have the student place it in the correct section of the menu.

Restaurant Charting Form

Name ______________________

DATE				
Small				
Medium				
Large				
Cold				
Hot				
Register				
Price				
Waiter				
Eat				
Drink				
Menu				
Fork				
Spoon				
Knife				
Straw				
Napkin				
Open				
Close				
Push				
Pull				
Yes				
No				
Please				
Thank you				

FINE MOTOR				
Opening Door				
Closing Door				
Cutting				
Coloring				
Handling Money				
Washing Dishes				
Folding Napkins				
Measuring				
Using Spoon				
Using Knife				
Using Fork				
Stirring				
Painting				
Using Straw				

VP = Verbal Prompt PP = Physical Prompt HH = Hand Over Hand + = Independent - = Incapable

Notes:

Restaurant
Related Materials

Books

Toad Eats Out by Susan Schade and Jon Buller. NY:Random House, Inc., 1995.
Curious George Goes to a Restaurant by Margret and H.A. Reys'. MA:Houghton Mifflin and Curgeo Agencies, Inc., 1988.
Frog Goes to Dinner by Mercer Mayer. NY:Dial Books, 1974.
Dinner at the Panda Palace by Stephanie Calmenson. NY:Harper Collins Publishers, 1991.
Pigs will be Pigs by Amy Axelrod. NY:Macmillan Publishing Co., 1994.
Richard Scarry's Busy Workers by Richard Scarry. WI:Western Publishing Co., Inc., 1987.
Eating Out by Helen Oxenbury. NY:Penguin Books USA, Inc., 1983.

Related Software

TouchMoney by Edmark
Fast Food/Restaurant Words by Edmark
My Town available through Edmark
Select-A-Meal Dictionary available through Edmark

Related Toys

Play food
Cash register
Play money
Apron
Play dishes
Menus

Supplemental Board
Restaurant Foods

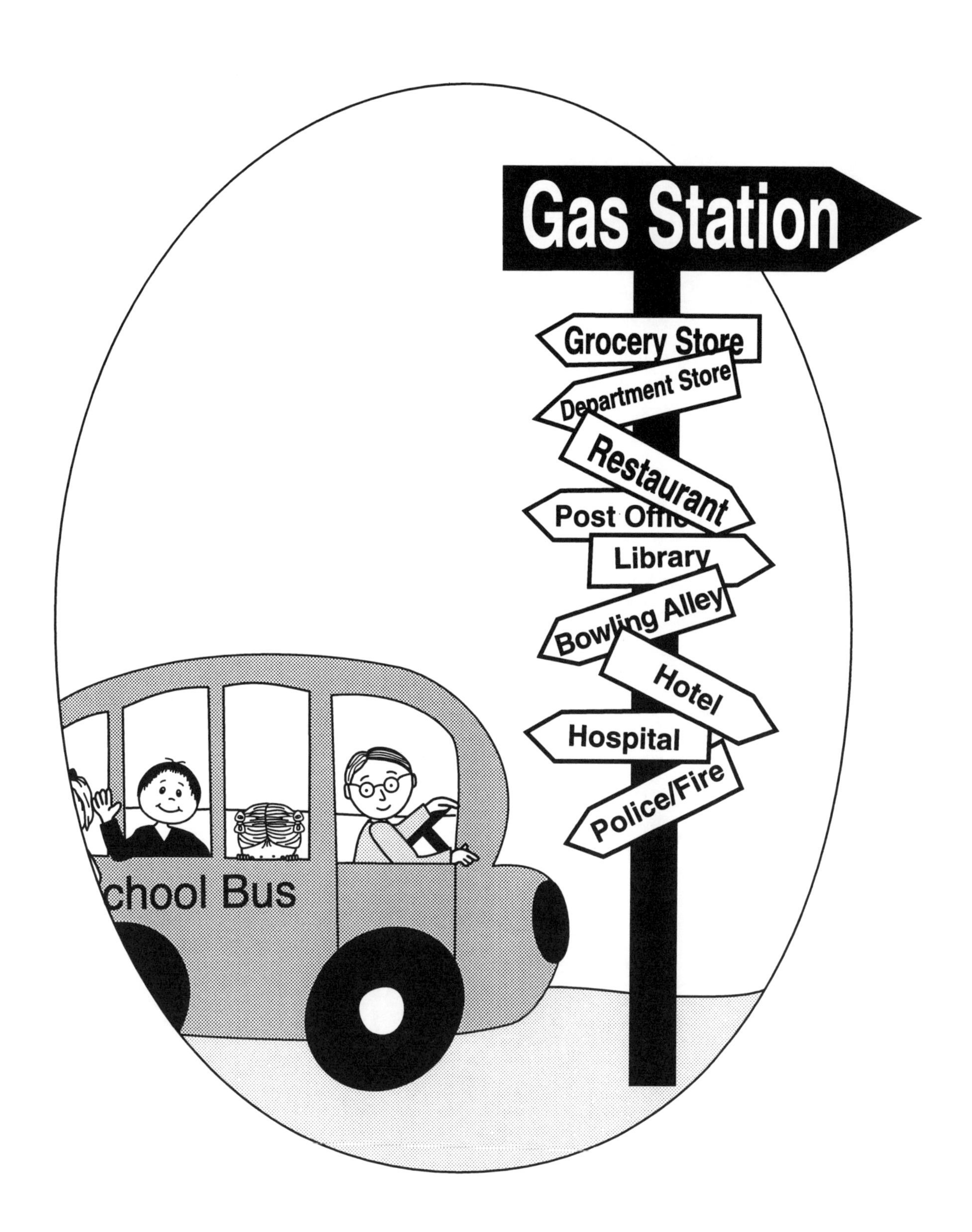
Gas Station
Grocery Store
Department Store
Restaurant
Post Offic
Library
Bowling Alley
Hotel
Hospital
Police/Fire
chool Bus

Gas Station

Getting Ready To Go

1. First tell your class where you are going on your trip and practice using your communication boards.
2. Discuss the behavior you expect (you may need to model appropriate behavior and do some role playing).
3. Designate responsibilities (see Job List, page 59).
4. Preprogram switches/augmentative communication devices to reflect the field trip you are taking.
5. Practice money skills.
6. Check to make sure all permission slips have been signed.
7. Grab the communication board and let's go!!!

Vocabulary List

color words	numbers	smooth	bumpy	big
little	wet	dry	middle	top
bottom	shelf	bag	register	price
clerk	open	close	push	pull
tires	snacks	gas	car	yes
no	please	thank you		

Language Skills

categorizing	labeling	identifying attributes
sentence structure	switch use	pragmatic skills

Fine Motor Skills

opening/closing doors	handling items	opening/closing coolers
handling money	carrying items	cutting
coloring	painting	pumping gas
twisting off lids	opening cans	cutting

Picture Vocabulary Words

Directions: Use the picture vocabulary words to review words and symbols that are new to your students.

Gas Station
Activities

Level I

1. Show your students the vehicle you arrived in. Ask them, *"What does our van need before it will work?"*
2. Show your students the gas tank. Ask them, *"What goes in this opening?"*
3. Have your students indicate yes/no to the following questions:
   "Do we eat this?" (Show them a magazine, toy, napkin, candy bar, etc.)
   "Is our van brown?" (Discuss colors before leaving the classroom and while noticing other vehicles.)

Level II

1. Have your students label the items found at the gas station. (*"What is this?"* Point to gas pump.) *"What do we do to the windshield? Where do we go to pay?"*
2. Ask your students what different items are made of. *"What is made out of metal? What is made out of rubber?"*
3. Have your students practice number concepts 0-5 using various items found at the gas station. *"How many tires are on the car? How many candy bars am I holding? How many sodas do I have?"*
4. Have your students practice manners and independence by making a purchase.
   Suggested sequence:
   "I need help. Please. 3 (items to be purchased). Thank you."

Level III

1. Have your students tell you where you plan to go and what you will find there. *"Where are we going today? What will we find there?"*
2. Have your students ask the price of an item found at the gas station.
   Suggested sequence:
   "I need help. Please. How much is it? 3 sodas. Thank you."
3. Have your students estimate the price of various items. *"How much would three gallons of gasoline cost us?"*
4. Have your students ask where the bathroom is located.
   Suggested sequence:
   "I need help. Please. Bathroom. Thank you."
5. Give your students directional cues when they are involved in life skills, such as pumping gas and/or washing the windows. *"Remember you have to squeeze the handle to make the gasoline come out. You have to push down hard when you are washing the windows."*

Gas Station — Level I
Communication Board

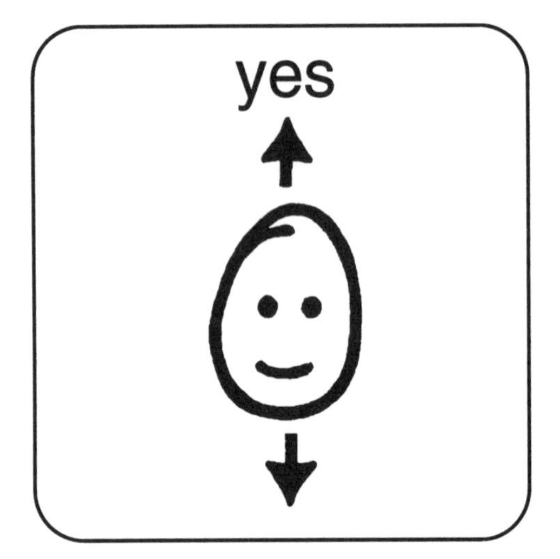

Gas Station — Level II
Communication Board

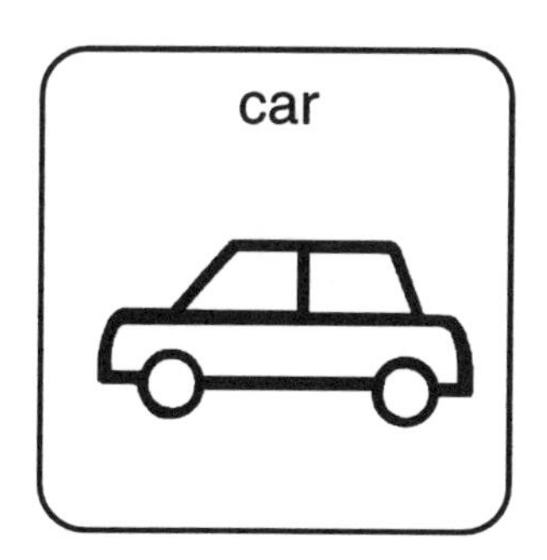

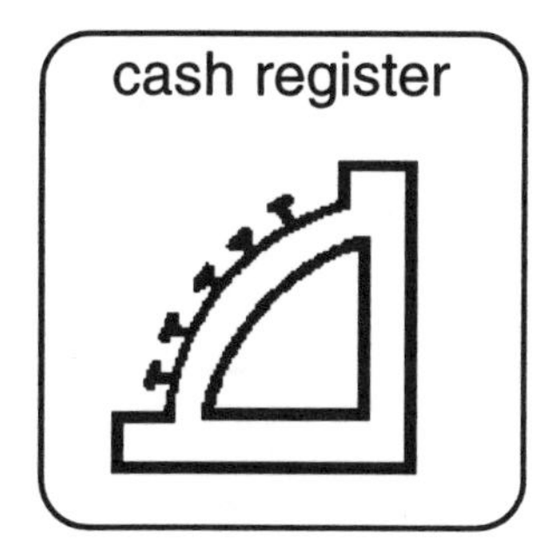

0 1 2 3 4 5

Gas Station — Level III
Communication Board

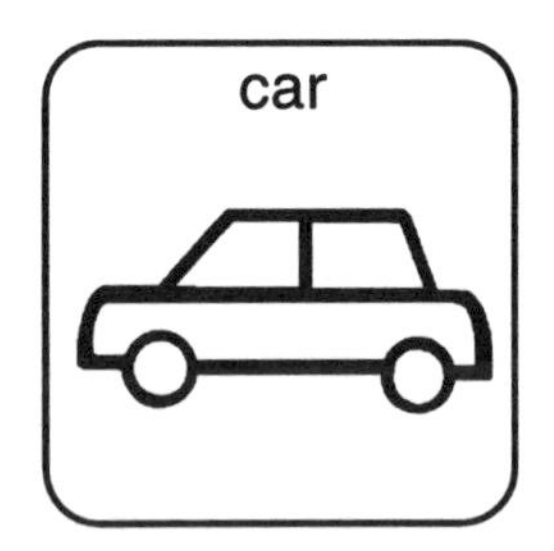

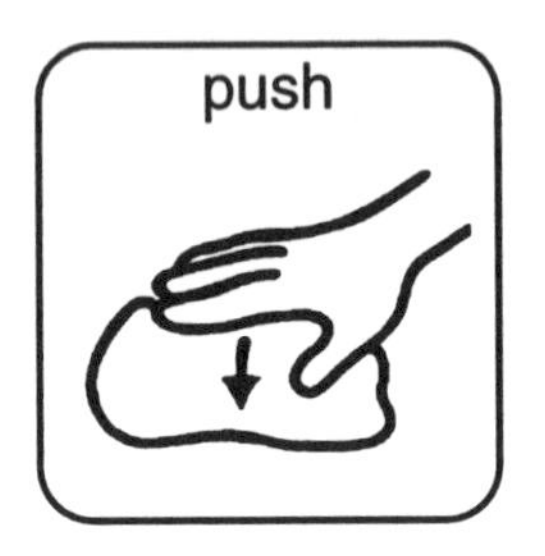

0	1	2	3	4	5	6	7	8	9

Gas Station
Follow-up Activities

Fine Motor & Follow-up Activities

 Practice role-playing cashier and attendant.

 Practice identifying and following basic signs.

 Track art (drive cars through paint and then on paper).

 Practice map skills.

 Practice washing windows.

Transition Activities for Older Students

- Pump gas.
- Wash windows and windshields.
- Wash cars.
- Sweep floors.
- Stock and dust shelves.
- Clean bathrooms.

All on-site work activities will initially require supervision. If your student is high functioning, this may eventually turn into an independent work situation. Refer to introduction regarding developing work sites, page I-7.

Gas Station Worksheet

Name:______________________________ Date:____________

1. Which item needs gasoline to work?

2. Which vehicle travels in the water?

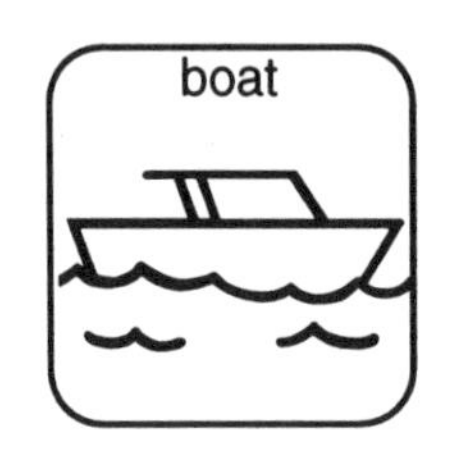

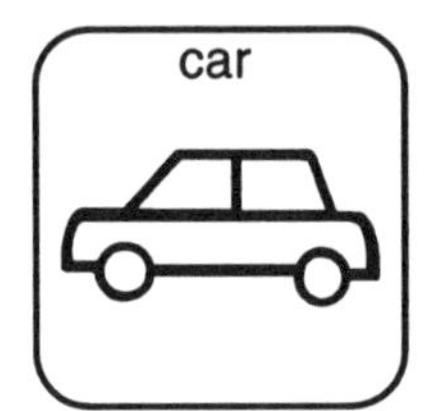

3. Which vehicle travels in the air?

4. What item is not part of a car?

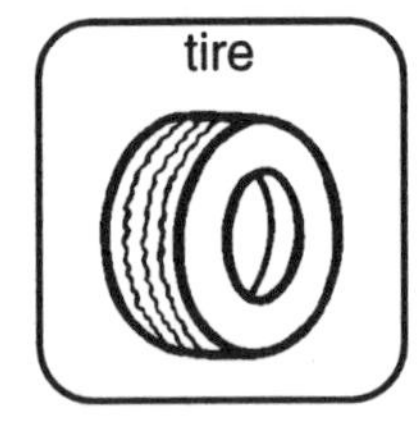

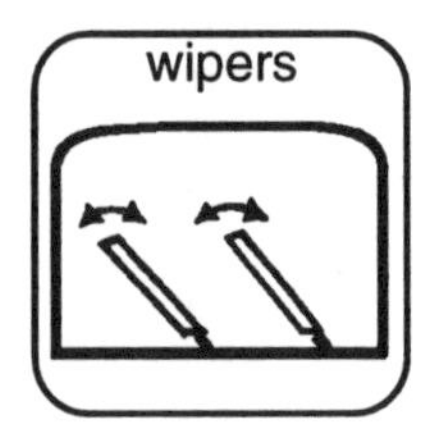

5. Which item is found at a convenience store?

Gas Station
Job List

Opening Doors ____________________

____

Operating Pump ____________________

____

Washing Windshields ____________________

____

Selecting Items ____________________

____

Handling Money ____________________

____

Carrying Items ____________________

____

Switches Programmed For ____________________

____

Gas Station Follow-up Activity

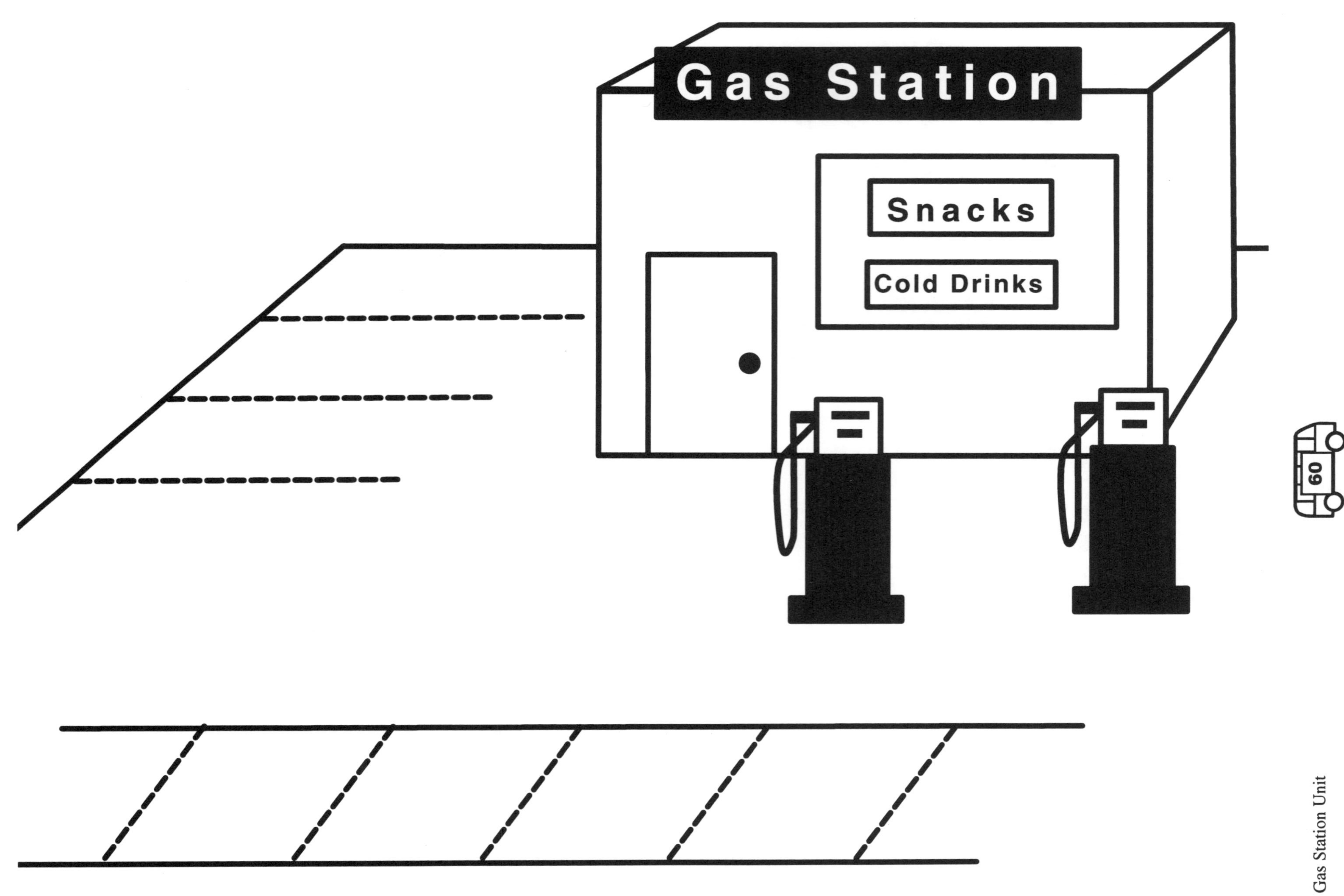

Gas Station Follow-up Activity Cutouts

Directions: The following items are to be used with the Gas Station Follow-up Activity, page 61. Duplicate both pages. Color, cut out, and laminate items on this page. Attach a reusable adhesive (such as Fun-Tak®) to the back of each item. In addition, color, and laminate the Gas Station Follow-up Activity page. Have the student determine if the item needs gas. As you say the name of the item, the student can place it either at the gas station or on the sidewalk.

Gas Station Charting Form

Name ______________________

DATE				
Big				
Smooth				
Bumpy				
Wet				
Dry				
Cold				
Up				
Down				
Middle				
Top				
Bottom				
Shelf				
Bag				
Register				
Price				
Clerk				
Open				
Close				
Push				
Pull				
Tires				
Snacks				
Gasoline				
Car				
Yes				
No				
Please				
Thank you				

FINE MOTOR				
Opening Door				
Closing Door				
Handling Items				
Opening Cooler				
Closing Cooler				
Handling Money				
Carrying Items				
Pumping Gas				
Opening Lids				
Opening Cans				
Cutting				
Coloring				
Painting				

VP = Verbal Prompt PP = Physical Prompt HH = Hand Over Hand + = Independent - = Incapable

Notes:

Gas Station

Related Materials

Books

An Auto Mechanic by Douglas Florian. NY:Greenwillow Books, 1991.
Cars by Daphne Butler. WI:Clarion Books, 1984.
Our World in Color, Things that Move by Arlene Rourke. FL:Silver Press, Inc., 1981.
Good Driving Amelia Bedelia by Herman Parish. NY:Greenwillow Books, 1995.
I Read Signs by Tana Hoban. NY: Greenwillow Books, 1983
Binky Gets a Car by Dick Gackenbach. NY:Clarion Books, 1993.
When I Ride in a Car by Dorothy Chlad. Canada:Regensteiner Publishing Enterprises, Inc., 1983.

Related Software

Signs Around You by Edmark
Looking for Words: Community available through Educational Resources

Related Toys

Toy vehicles
Toy gas pump
Road signs
Roadway rug or mat

Post Office
Grocery Store
Department Store
Restaurant
Gas Station
Library
Bowling Alley
Hotel
Hospital
Police/Fire
School Bus

Post Office

Getting Ready To Go

1. First tell your class where you are going on your trip and practice using your communication boards.
2. Discuss the behavior you expect (you may need to model appropriate behavior and do some role playing).
3. Bring nonsense item (empty soda can).
4. Bring letters from your classroom to mail.
5. Bring small package from your classroom for making comparisons.
6. Designate responsibilities (see Job List, page 75).
7. Preprogram switches/augmentative communication devices to reflect the field trip you are taking.
8. Work on money skills.
9. Check to make sure all permission slips have been signed.
10. Grab the communication board and let's go!!!

Vocabulary List

color words	numbers	big	little	heavy
up	down	middle	top	bottom
price	open	close	push	pull
envelope	mail	stamp	package	yes
no	please	thank you		

Language Skills

categorizing	labeling	identifying attributes
sentence structure	switch use	pragmatic skills

Fine Motor Skills

opening/closing doors	handling items	handling money
cutting	licking stamps	writing
folding paper	wrapping packages	opening mail
using keys		

Picture Vocabulary Words

Directions: Use the picture vocabulary words to review words and symbols that are new to your students.

Post Office
Activities

Level I

1. Show your students a letter without a stamp and have them use their communication board to indicate what is missing. *"What needs to be on our letter before we can mail it?"*
2. Show your students the letter and ask them, *"Where do we put our letters that we want to mail?"*
3. Have your students indicate yes/no to the following questions:
   "Do we have to put a stamp on a letter before we mail it?" (Show your students a letter you addressed in class.)
   "Do we put trash in the mailbox?" (Show the children an empty soda can.)
   "Will this item fit in the mailbox?" (Show the children a letter and a package.)

Level II

1. Show your students different items associated with the post office, such as a package, letter, stamp, and envelope. Ask them, *"What is this?"*
2. Have your students practice number concepts 0-5 by having your students count the number of items you are planning to mail or that you have received. *"How many items did we get in the mail today? How many letters are we sending?"*
3. Have your students use their communication board to indicate which item is heavier/bigger using letters and packages. *"Which one is heavier? Which one is bigger?"*
4. Have your students purchase stamps using their communication board.
   Suggested sequence:
   "I need help. 2 stamps. Please. Thank you."
5. Show your students the different types of mailboxes. Ask them, *"What would you use to open this box?"*

Level III

1. Have your students tell you where you plan to go and what you will find there. *"Where are we going today? What will we find there?"*
2. Have your students estimate the cost of possible items purchased. *"How much would 4 stamps cost?"*
3. Ask your students about the information found on a letter. *"What tells us where the mail is going?"*
4. Show your students various pieces of mail. Ask them which mailbox they should go in. *"Would this go in the local or out-of-town box?"*
5. Have your students mail a package. Have them use their communication board to ask how much it would cost to mail a package.
   Suggested sequence:
   "I need help. Please. How much is it? Mail. Package. Thank you."
6. Have your students purchase stamps using their communication board.
   Suggested sequence:
   "I need help. 2 stamps. Please. Thank you."

Post Office — Level I Communication Board

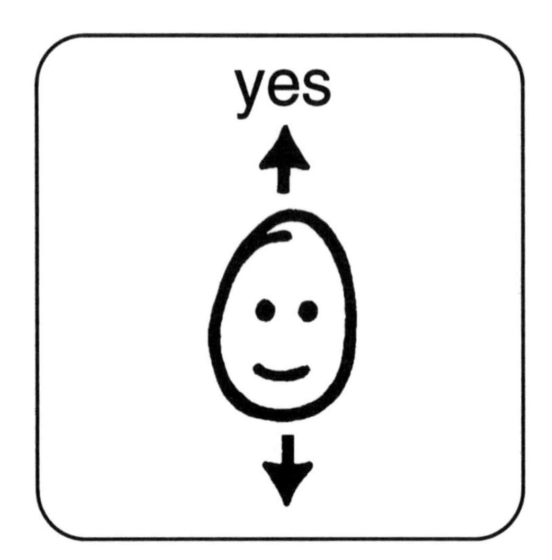

Post Office — Level II Communication Board

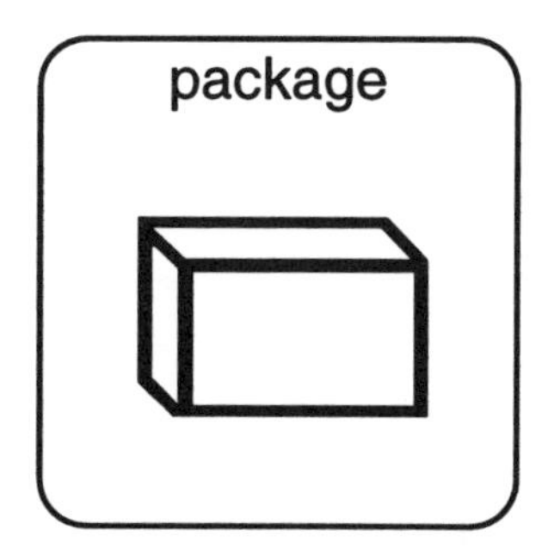

0 1 2 3 4 5

Post Office — Level III
Communication Board

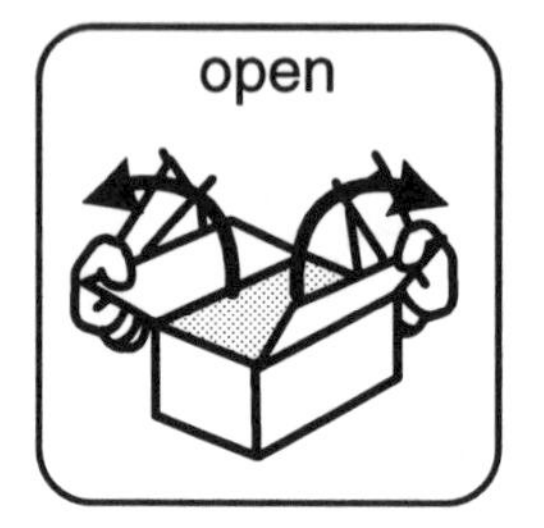

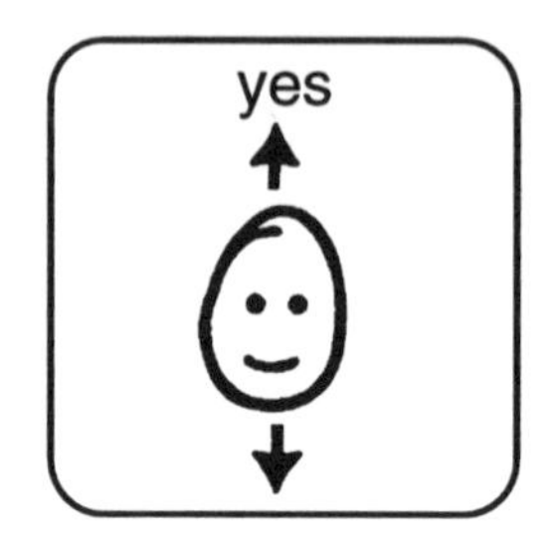

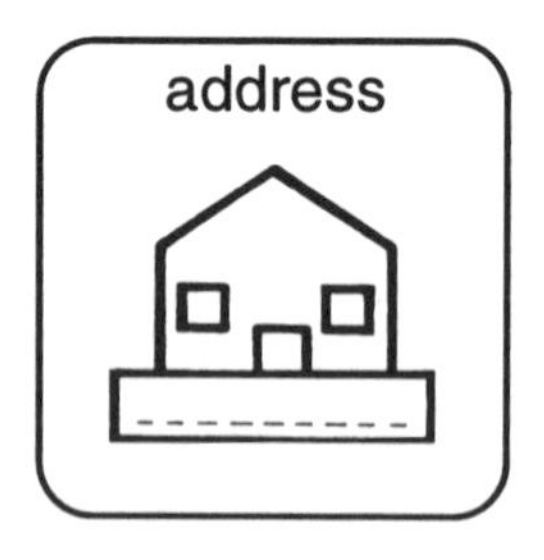

0	1	2	3	4	5	6	7	8	9

Post Office
Follow-up Activities

Fine Motor & Follow-up Activities

Practice licking stamps and envelopes.

Practice writing letters (letter formation, format, etc.)

Practice stuffing envelopes (trifold, alignment, etc.).

Practice collating papers and sorting.

Start collecting stamps. Have your students cut used stamps off of envelopes.

Stamp art.

Transition Activities for Older Students

- Clean the post office:
  - Sweep / mop floors.
  - Clean counters.
  - Wash windows.
- Provide a package wrapping service for customers.
- Provide pick up and delivery services for businesses.
- Wash delivery vehicles.
- Newspaper route.

All on-site work activities will initially require supervision. If your student is high functioning, this may eventually turn into an independent work situation. Refer to introduction regarding developing work sites, page I-7.

Post Office Worksheet

Name:______________________________ Date:____________

1. What do you put on the envelope before you mail your letter?

2. What do you put the letter in before you mail it?

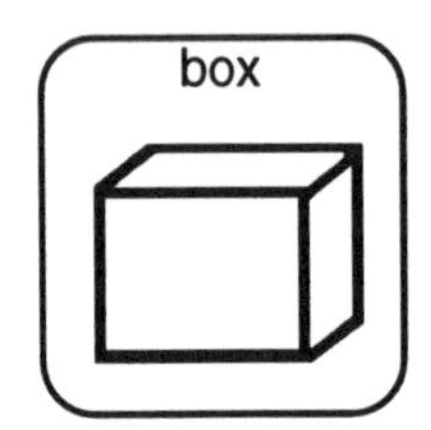

3. Who delivers your mail?

4. Where do you go to mail a letter?

5. Which item will cost the most to mail?

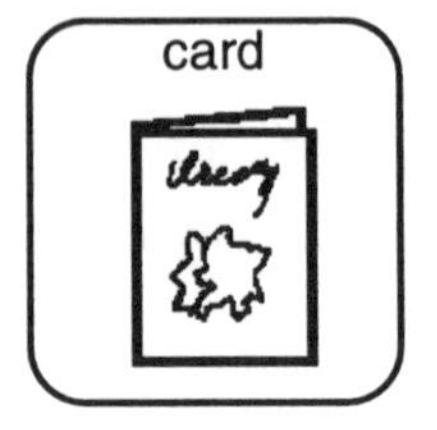

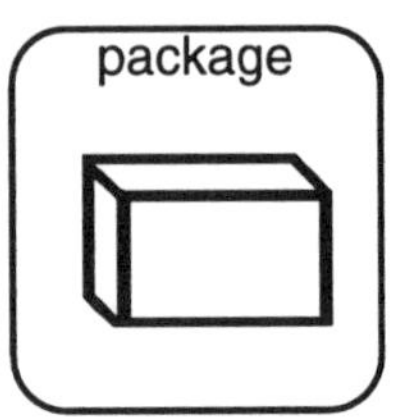

Post Office
Job List

Opening Doors ______________________

____

Opening Mailbox ______________________

____

Purchasing Stamps ______________________

____

Stamping Letters ______________________

____

Mailing Letters/Packages ______________________

____

Switches Programmed For ______________________

____

Post Office Follow-up Activity Envelope

4

Directions: Cut out envelope. Fold UP tabs 1 and 2 on the dotted lines. Apply glue to the top side of the tabs. Fold UP flap 3 and secure to the glued flaps. Fold DOWN flap 4. Use glue to seal envelope once card has been inserted.

1

2

3

Post Office Follow-up Activity Card

Directions: Cut out card. Cut and paste labels on the card. Personalize and decorate your card. Fold and place in envelope.

Dear____________,

From ____________

Post Office Charting Form

Name ____________________________

DATE				
Big				
Little				
Up				
Down				
Middle				
Top				
Bottom				
Heavy				
Price				
Open				
Close				
Push				
Pull				
Envelope				
Mail				
Stamp				
Package				
Yes				
No				
Please				
Thank you				

FINE MOTOR				
Opening Door				
Closing Door				
Cutting				
Handling Mail				
Handling Money				
Licking Stamps				
Writing				
Folding Paper				
Wrapping Boxes				
Opening Mail				
Using Keys				

VP = Verbal Prompt PP = Physical Prompt HH = Hand Over Hand + = Independent - = Incapable

Notes:

Post Office
Related Materials

Books

I want to be a Postman by Carla Greene. USA:Children's Press, 1963.
The Post Office Book, Mail and How it Moves by Gail Gibbons. NY:Thomas Y. Crowell, 1982.
Mailbox Quailbox by Margaret Ronay Legum. Canada:Collier Macmillan Canada, Inc., 1985.
First Class! The Postal System in Action by Harold Roth. NY:Random House, Inc., 1983.
Where Does the Mail Go? by Melvin and Gilda Berger. TN:Ideals Children's Books, 1994.
Richard Scarry's Busy Workers by Richard Scarry. WI:Western Publishing Co., Inc., 1987.

Related Software

Work Processing Progam

Related Toys

Student mail center
Envelopes
Stamps
Ink pad
Paper

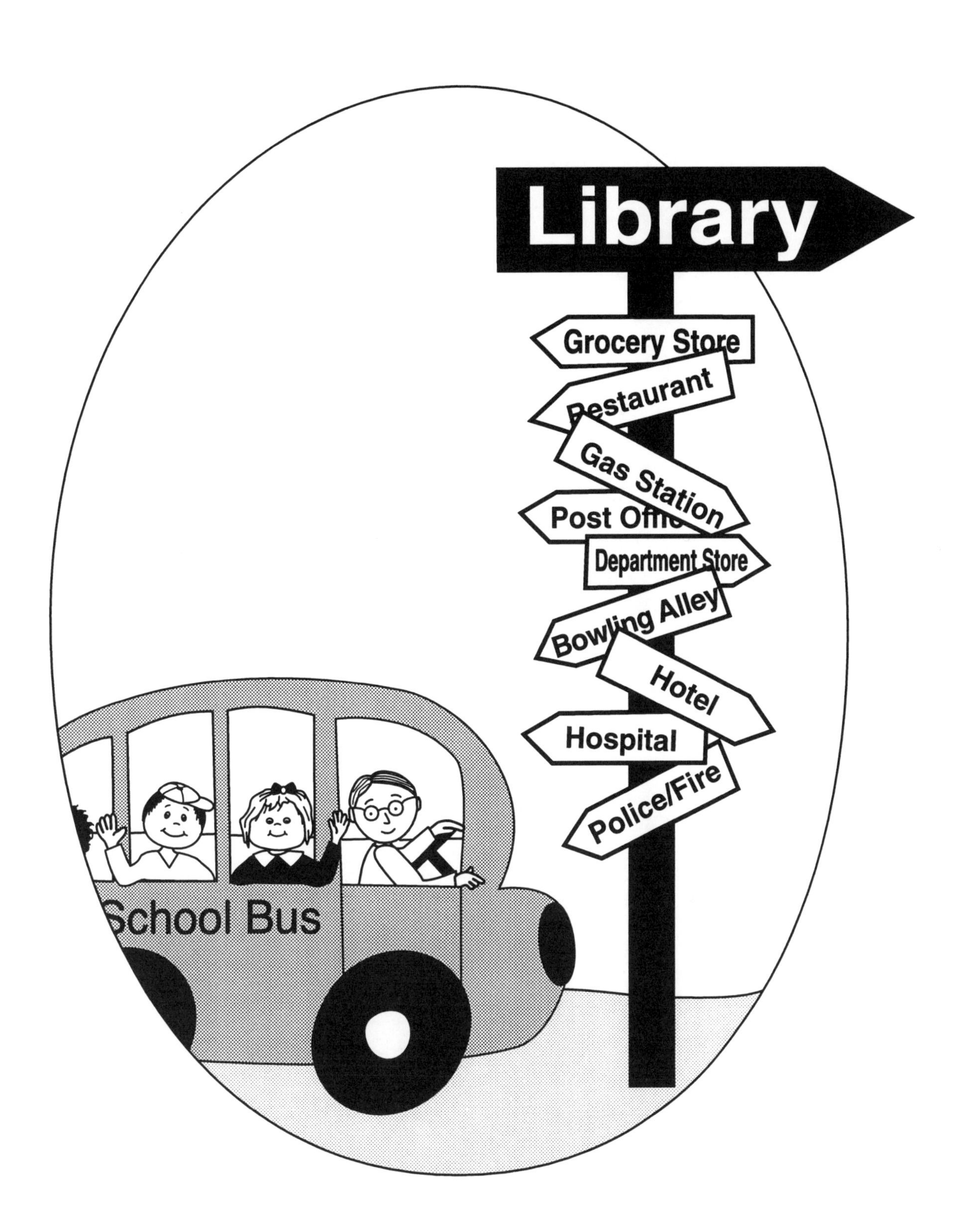
Library
Grocery Store
Restaurant
Gas Station
Department Store
Bowling Alley
Hotel
Hospital
Police/Fire
School Bus

Library

Getting Ready To Go

1. First tell your class where you are going on your trip and practice using your communication boards.
2. Discuss the behavior you expect (you may need to model appropriate behavior and do some role playing).
3. Bring a copy of a favorite book from your classroom.
4. Take students' library cards (If your students don't have library cards, be sure to get them.)
5. Designate responsibilities (see Job List page 91).
6. Preprogram switches/augmentative communication devices to reflect the field trip you are taking.
7. Check to make sure all permission slips have been signed.
8. Grab your communication board and let's go!!!

Vocabulary List

book	video tape	cassette	color words	numbers
same	different	big	little	heavy
up	down	middle	top	bottom
shelf	open	close	push	pull
yes	no	please	thank you	

Language Skills

categorizing	labeling	identifying attributes
sentence structure	switch use	pragmatic skills

Fine Motor Skills

opening/closing doors	handling books	carrying books
turning pages	stamping	operating VCR
operating tape recorder	cutting	coloring

Picture Vocabulary Words

Directions: Use the picture vocabulary words to review words and symbols that are new to your students.

Library Activities

Level I

1. Show your students different items available for check-out at the library. Have them use their communication boards to categorize books and tapes. *"Is this a book or a tape?"*
2. Discuss the functions of books and tapes with your students. State the functions and have them indicate the corresponding item. *"What do we read? What do we need to use a cassette player with?"*
3. Have your students indicate yes/no to the following questions:
   "Can we yell in the library?" (Discuss appropriate behavior.)
   "Can we stand on the tables?" (Discuss appropriate behavior.)
   "Are these books the same?" (Find multiple copies of the same book at the library or bring a favorite book from your classroom.)

Level II

1. Have your students label items found in the library. Ask them, *"What is this?"*
2. Have your students practice number concepts 0-5 using books, tapes, and videos. *"How many books am I holding?"*
3. Have your students indicate their choice between items using their communication boards. *"Which one do you want?"*
4. Have your students bring the title of their favorite book to the library. Have them ask the librarian for help in locating that book.
   Suggested sequence:
   "I need help. Please. I want that one. Thank you."
5. Have your students tell you what we do with a book when you are done with it or have them ask the librarian where the book return is.
   Suggested sequence:
   "I need help. Please. Book return. Thank you."
6. Have your students get a library card of their own. Discuss why you need one.

Level III

1. Have your students tell you where you plan to go and what you will find there. *"Where are we going today? What will we find there?"*
2. Have your students categorize books into their appropriate section. *"This is a true story. Where would this book be found?"*
3. Have your students use their communication boards to answer the following questions:
   "What do we need to check out a book?"
   "Which is heavier/bigger?" (Show students different books and tapes.)
   "How many books did we check out/return?"
   "Are these books the same?"
4. Have your students engage in conversation relating to their interest, likes, and dislikes using their communication boards. *"Do you think you would enjoy this book/movie/tape?"*
5. Have your students ask where the bathroom is located.
   Suggested sequence:
   "I need help. Please. Bathroom. Thank you."

Library — Level I
Communication Board

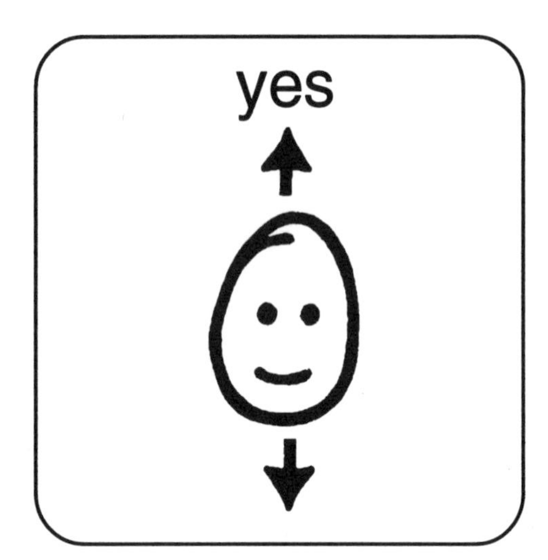

Library — Level II
Communication Board

book

tape

movie

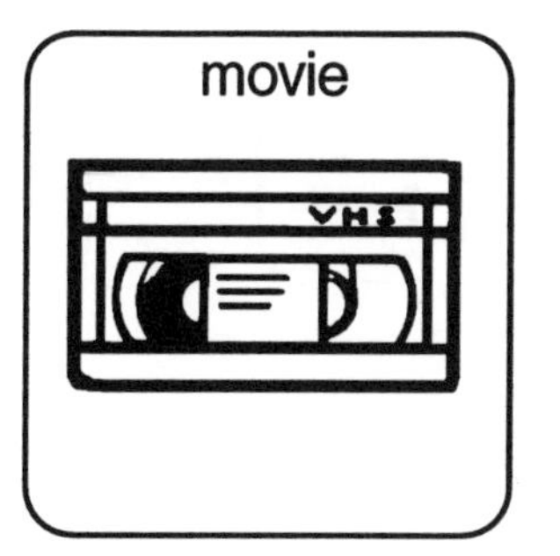

library card

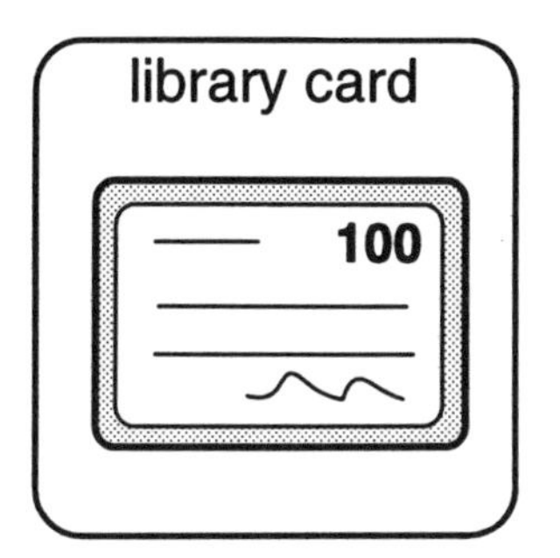

I want that one

book return

I need help

please

thank you

0

2 3 4 5

Library — Level III Communication Board

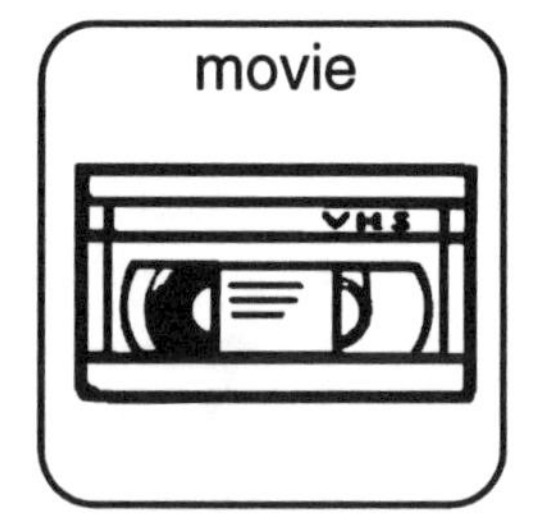

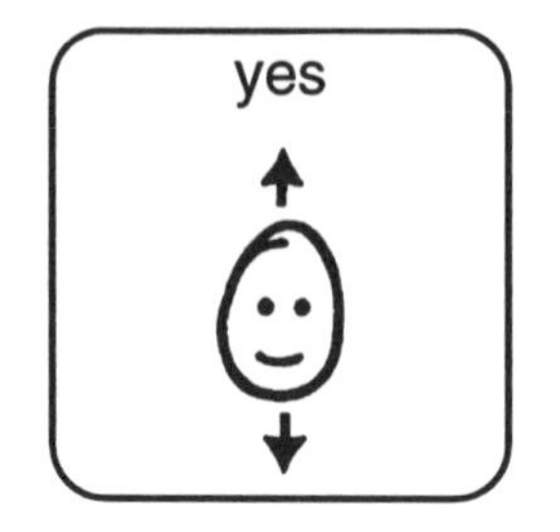

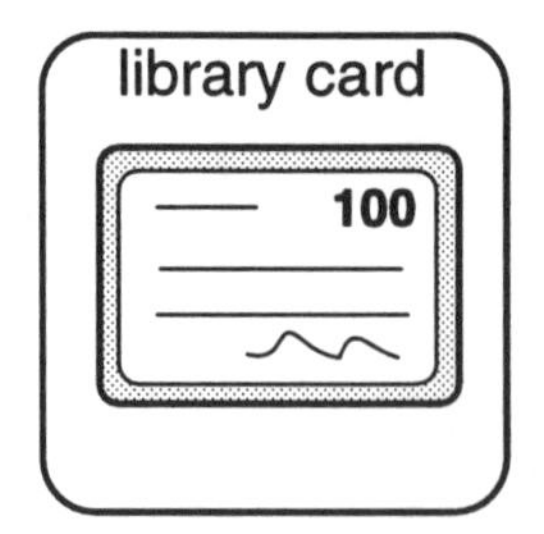

0	1	2	3	4	5	6	7	8	9

Library
Follow-up Activities

Fine Motor & Follow-up Activities

ABC Alphabetizing activities.

 Practice independent operation of television, VCR, and tape recorder.

 Make your own books by cutting out pictures from magazines.

 Role-play librarian duties.

 Stamp art.

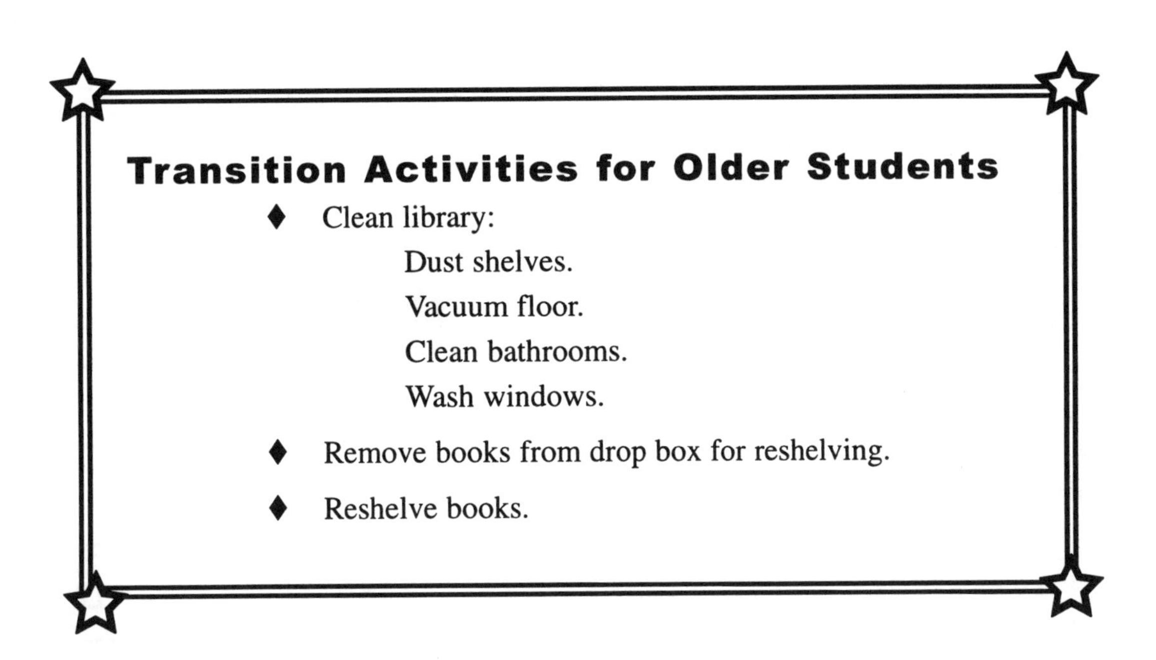

Transition Activities for Older Students

- Clean library:
  - Dust shelves.
  - Vacuum floor.
  - Clean bathrooms.
  - Wash windows.
- Remove books from drop box for reshelving.
- Reshelve books.

All of the work activities will initially require supervision. If your student is high functioning, this may eventually turn into an independent work situation. Refer to introduction regarding developing work sites, page I-7.

Library Worksheet

Name:______________________________ Date:______________

1. Where do we go to check out books?

2. Where do we keep our books?

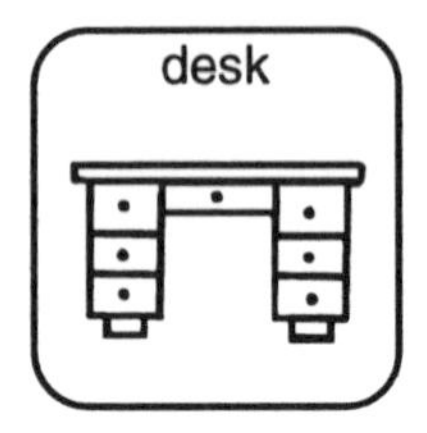

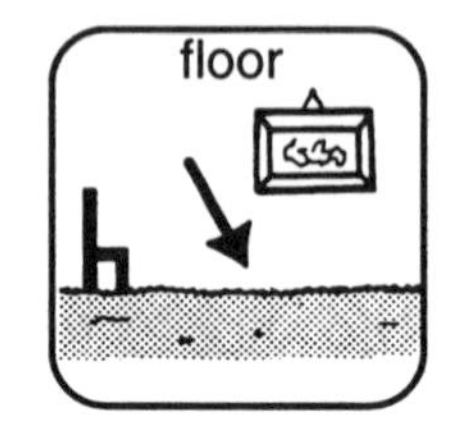

3. Who can help us read our book?

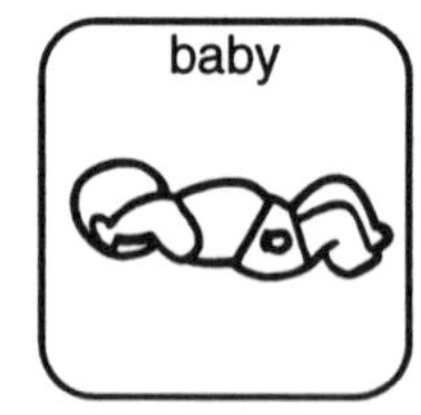

4. What do we use to play our books on tape?

5. Which item is not found at the library?

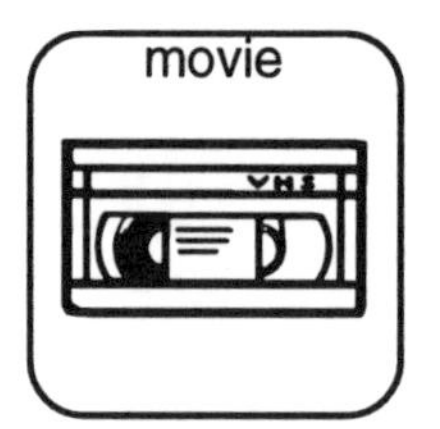

Library
Job List

Opening Doors ______________________

____

Selecting Books ______________________

____

Selecting Movies ______________________

____

Selecting Audio Tapes ______________________

____

Handling Library Cards ______________________

____

Pushing in Chairs ______________________

____

Carrying Books ______________________

____

Switches Programmed For ______________________

____

Library Follow-up Activity

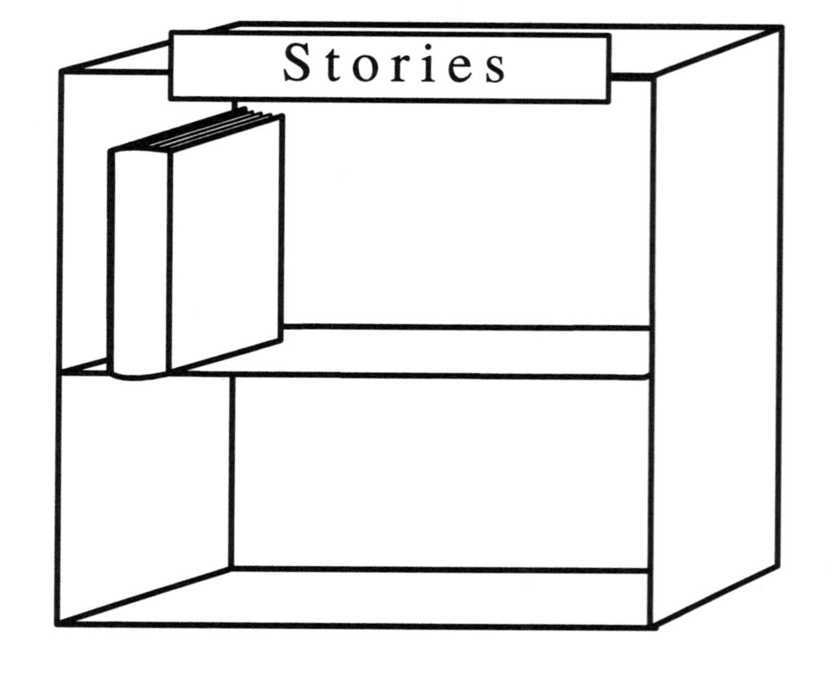

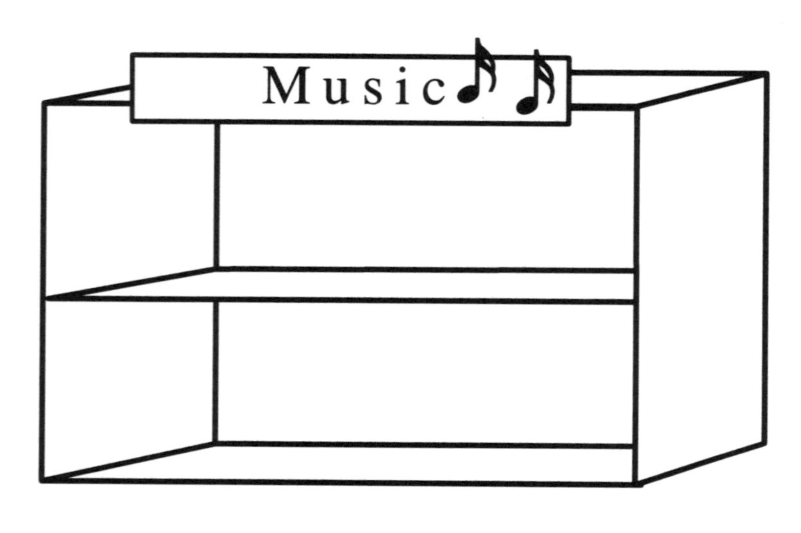

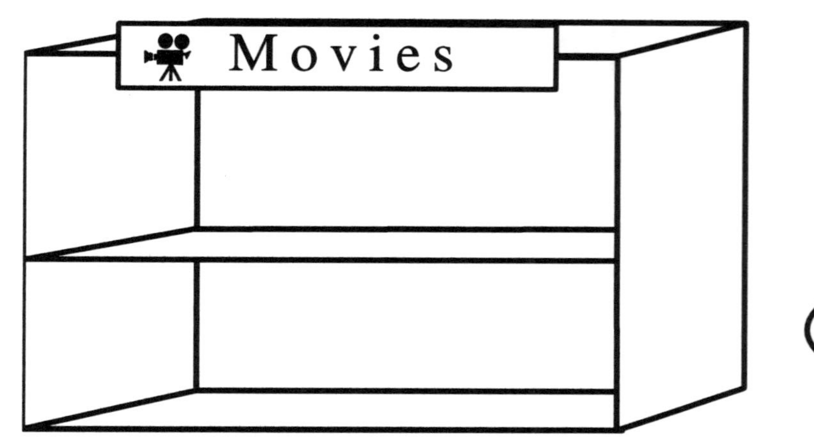

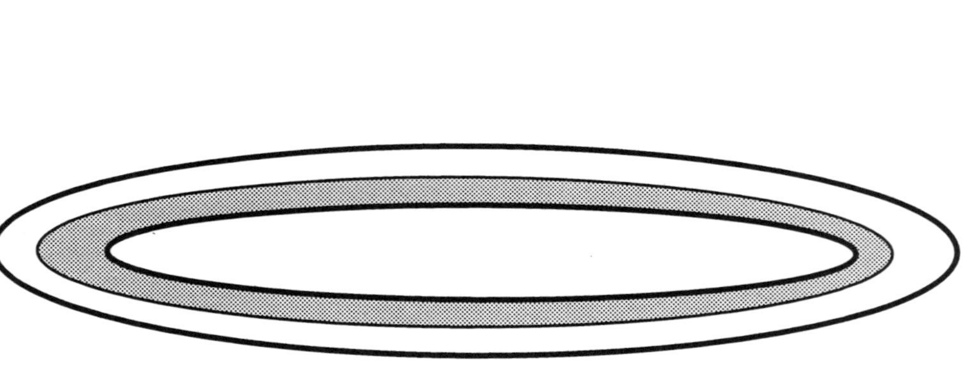

Library Follow-up Activity Cutouts

Directions: The following items are to be used with the Library Follow-up Activity, page 92. Duplicate both pages. Color, cut out, and laminate items on this page. Attach a reusable adhesive (such as Fun-Tak®) to the back of each item. In addition, color, and laminate the master Library Follow-up Activity page. As you say the name of the item, have the student place the item in the correct area of the library.

Library Charting Form

Name ______________________

DATE				
Big				
Little				
Same				
Different				
Heavy				
Up				
Down				
Middle				
Top				
Bottom				
Shelf				
Open				
Close				
Push				
Pull				
Yes				
No				
Book				
Video Tape				
Cassette				
Please				
Thank you				

FINE MOTOR				
Opening Door				
Closing Door				
Cutting				
Coloring				
Handling Books				
Carrying Books				
Turning Pages				
Stamping				
Using VCR				
Using TV				
Tape Recorder				

VP=Verbal Prompt PP=Physical Prompt HH=Hand Over Hand + = Independent - = Incapable

Notes:

Library
Related Materials

Books

The Library by Sarah Stewart. Canada: Harper Collins Canada Ltd, 1995.
I Took My Frog to the Library by Eric A. Kimmel. NY:Penguin Books, 1990.
Teeny Witch Goes to the Library by Liz Matthews. NJ:Troll Associates, 1991.
Molly at the Library by Ruth Shaw Radlauer. NY:Simon & Schuster, 1988.
A Visit to the Sesame Street Library by Deborah Hautzig. NY:Random House, Inc., 1986.
50 Games to Play in the Library or Classroom by Carol K. Lee and Fay Edwards. WV:Alleyside Press, 1988.
Harry in Trouble by Barbara Ann Porte. NY:Greenwillow Books, 1989.

Related Software

Stanley's Sticker Stories by Edmark
Community Exploration available through Edmark
Big Book Marker: Letters, Number and Shapes available through Cambridge Development Laboratory
Storybook Maker Deluxe available through Cambridge Development Laboratory

Related Toys

Student mail center
Envelopes
Stamps
Ink pad
Paper

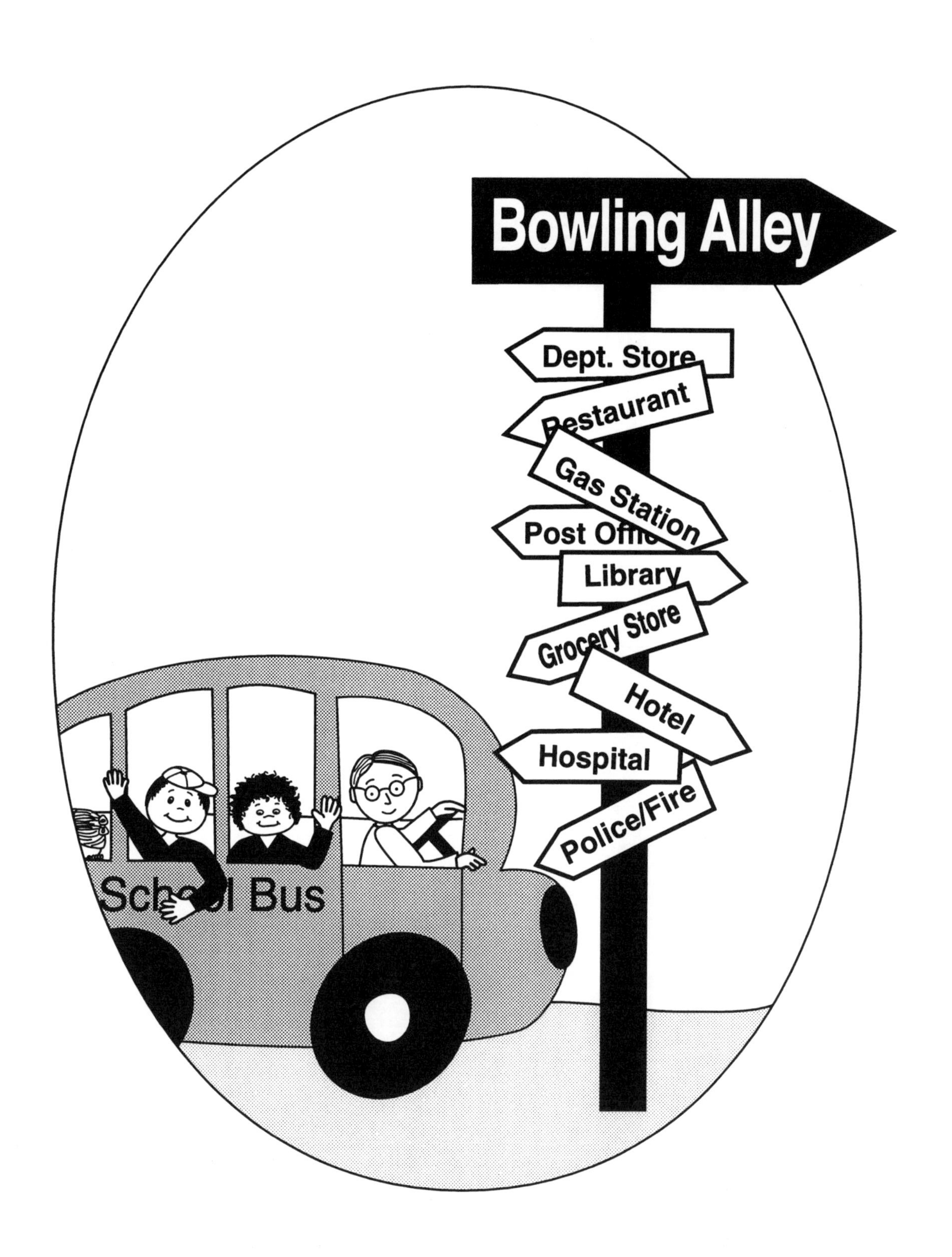
Bowling Alley
Dept. Store
Restaurant
Gas Station
Library
Grocery Store
Hotel
Hospital
Police/Fire
School Bus

Bowling Alley

Getting Ready To Go

1. First tell your class where you are going on your trip and practice using your communication boards.
2. Discuss the behavior you expect (you may need to model appropriate behavior and do some role playing).
3. Determine students' shoe sizes.
4. Practice tying shoes.
5. Designate responsibilities (see Job List page 107).
6. Preprogram switches/augmentative communication devices to reflect the field trip you are taking.
7. Practice money skills.
8. Check to make sure all permission slips have been signed.
9. Grab the communication boards and let's go!!!

Vocabulary List

color words	numbers	shapes	roll	pin
bowling ball	shoes	lane	spare	strike
big	little	price	clerk	open
close	push	pull	yes	no
please	thank you			

Language Skills

categorizing	labeling	identifying attributes
sentence structure	switch use	pragmatic skills
turn-taking skills		

Fine Motor Skills

opening/closing doors	tying shoes	writing
operating vending machines	holding bowling ball	using spray can
handling money	cutting	coloring

Bowling Alley
Picture Vocabulary Words

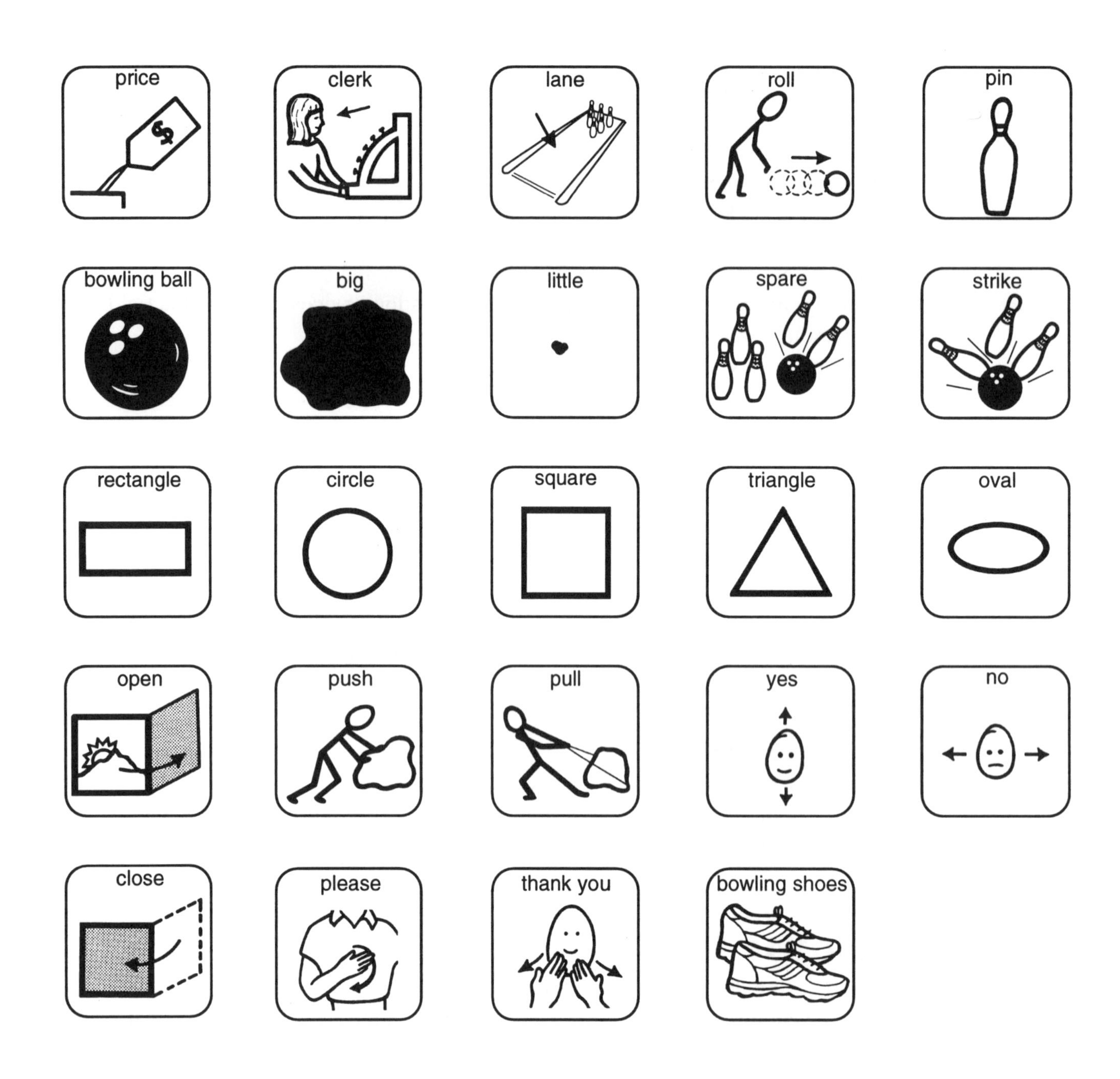

Directions: Use the picture vocabulary words to review words and symbols that are new to your students.

Bowling Alley
Activities

Level I

1. Ask your students, *"What do we roll down the lane?"* as you are walking around the bowling alley.
2. Ask your students, *"What are we trying to knock down?"*
3. Have your students indicate yes/no to the following questions:
   "Do we bounce a bowling ball?" (Show the students a bowling ball.)
   "Do we sleep at the bowling alley?" (Pretend to go to sleep.)
   "Do we take turns bowling?" (Discuss bowling rules.)

Level II

1. Have your students label items found in the bowling alley showing them shoes, pins, and bowling ball. Ask them, *"What is this?"*
2. Have your students practice the concept of turn taking while you are bowling. Have your students use their communication board to indicate whose turn it is. *"Now whose turn is it?"*
3. Ask your students, *"What do we do with the bowling ball? What are we trying to knock down?"*
4. Have your students ask the attendant for help in renting shoes.
   Suggested sequence:
   "I need help. Please. Shoes. . .5 (size). Thank you."
5. Have your students practice number concepts 0-5 by asking your students the following questions: *"How many holes are there in a bowling ball? How many bowling balls/pins do you see?"*

Level III

1. Have your students tell you where you plan to go and what you will find there. *"Where are we going today? What will we find there?"*
2. Have your students ask the attendant for help getting a scorecard and paying for a game.
   Suggested sequence:
   "I need help. Scorecard. How much is it? Please. Thank you."
3. Have your students estimate the cost of four people bowling a game. *"How much would it cost for all four of us to bowl?"*
4. Have your students estimate the size of shoe they wear after telling them your size. *"What size bowling shoe do you think you wear?"*
5. Have your students practice the concept of turn taking while you are bowling. Have your students use their communication board to indicate whose turn it is. *"Now whose turn is it?"*
6. Have your students ask where the bathroom is located.
   Suggested sequence:
   "I need help. Please. Bathroom. Thank you."

Bowling Alley — Level I Communication Board

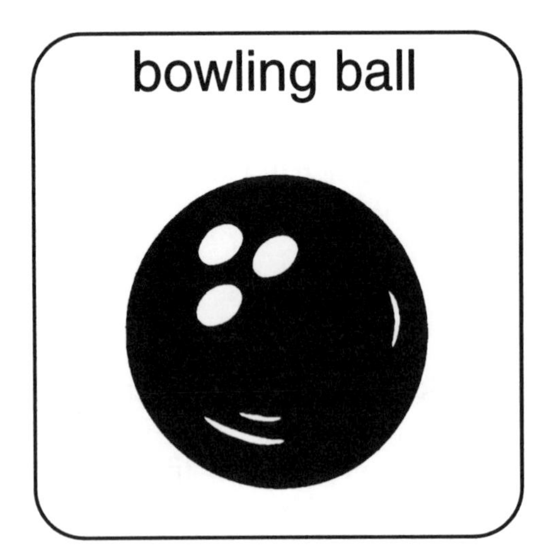

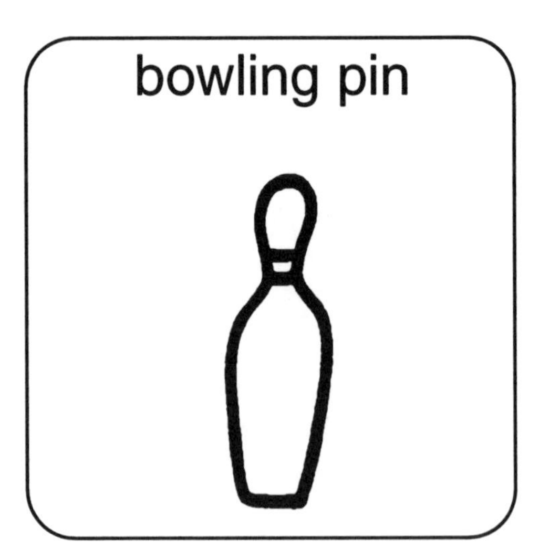

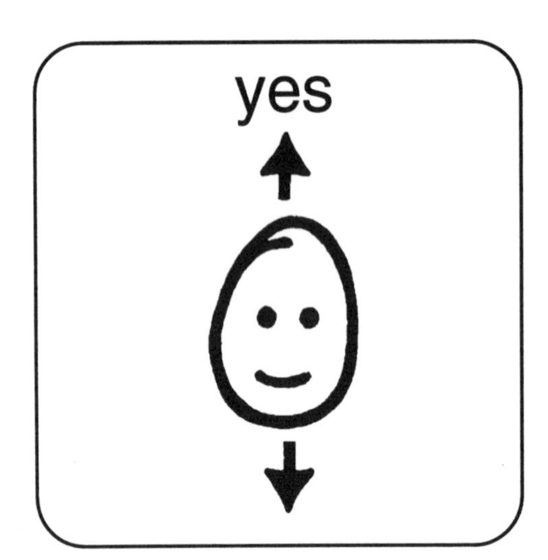

Bowling Alley — Level II
Communication Board

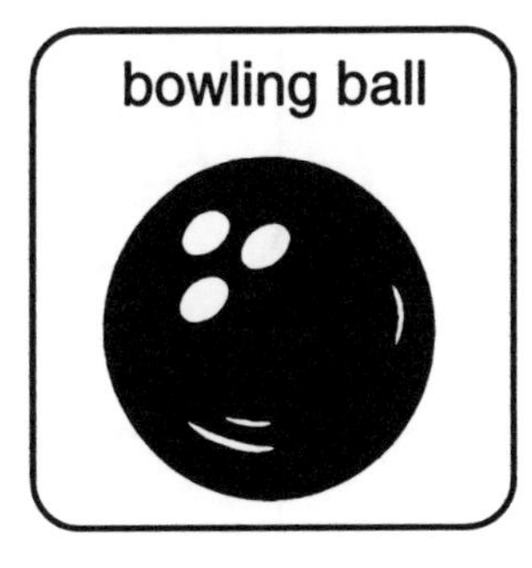

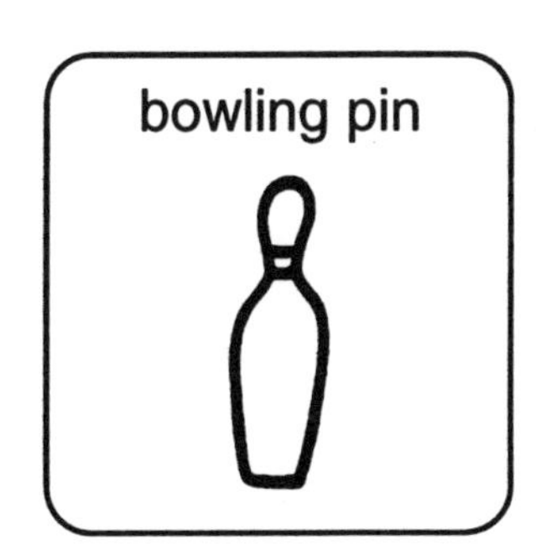

0

2 3 4 5

Bowling Alley — Level III Communication Board

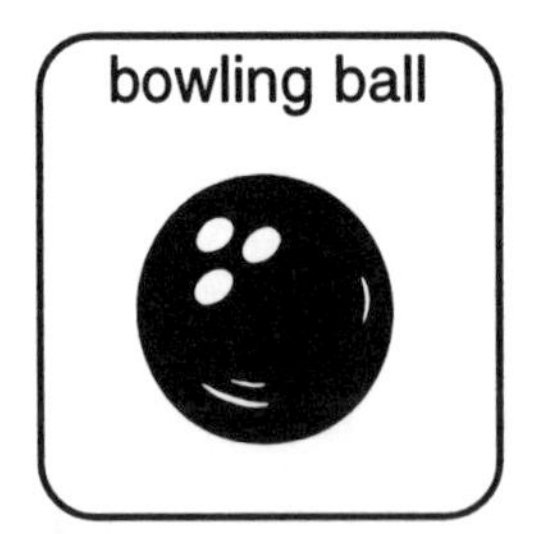

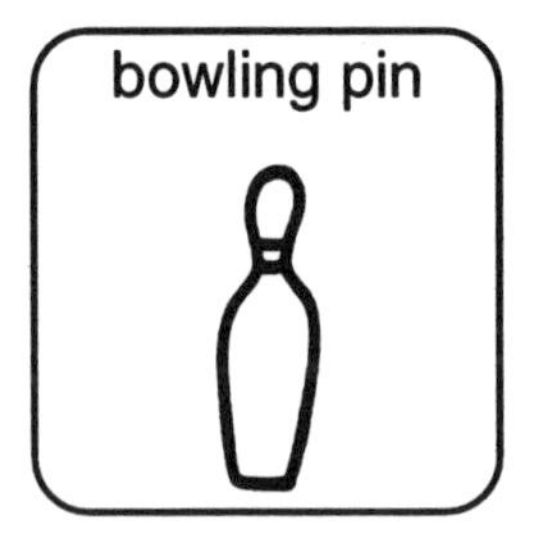

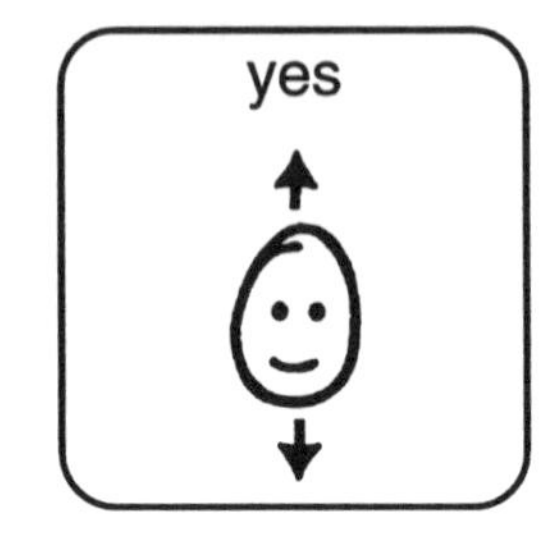

How much is it?

? $

0	1	2	3	4	5	6	7	8	9

Bowling Alley
Follow-up Activities

Fine Motor & Follow-up Activities

 Practice shoe tying.

 Role-play with play bowling set.

 Practice turn taking.

 Shape art. (Cut out different shapes from construction paper and magazines to create a collage.)

 Practice number order and sequencing.

 Practice math skills by keeping score.

Transition Activities for Older Students

- Sweep floors.
- Load vending machines.
- Clean alley.
- Clean bathrooms.
- Disinfect shoes.
- Wash bowling balls.
- Wash off score tables and chairs.
- Practice checkbook management.

All on-site work activities will initially require supervision. If your student is high functioning, this may eventually turn into an independent work situation. Refer to introduction regarding developing work sites, page I-7.

Bowling Alley Worksheet

Name:______________________________ Date:____________

1. What shoes do you wear when you bowl?

2. What shape is a bowling ball?

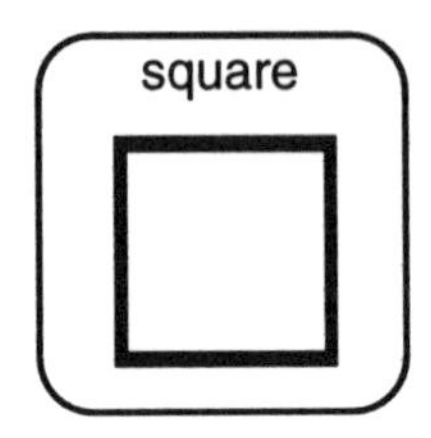

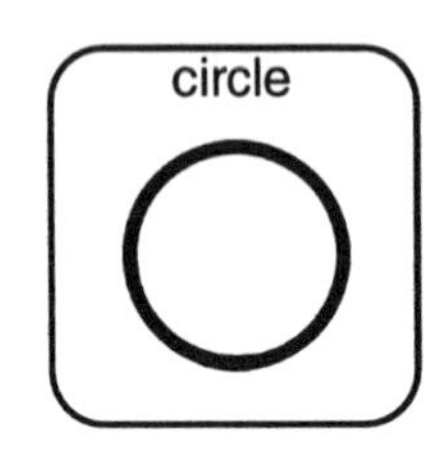

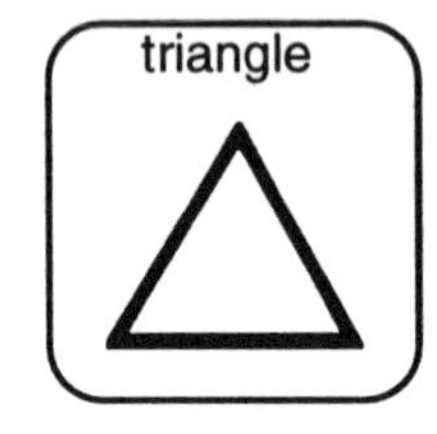

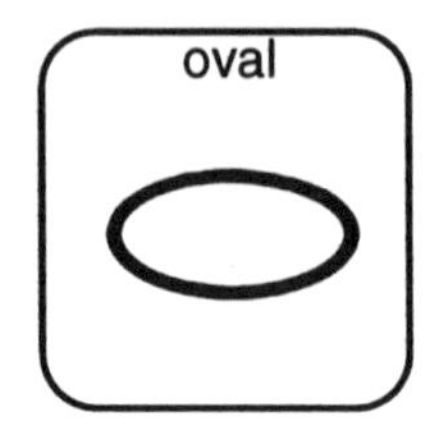

3. What do you do with the bowling ball?

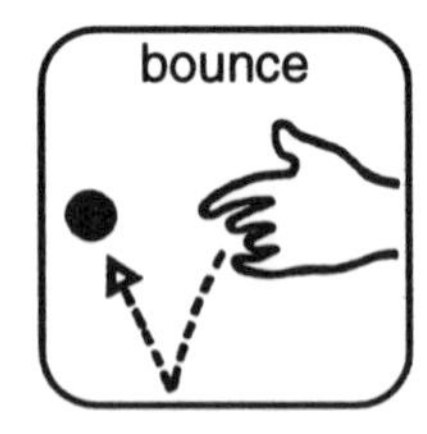

4. What kind of ball do you use for bowling?

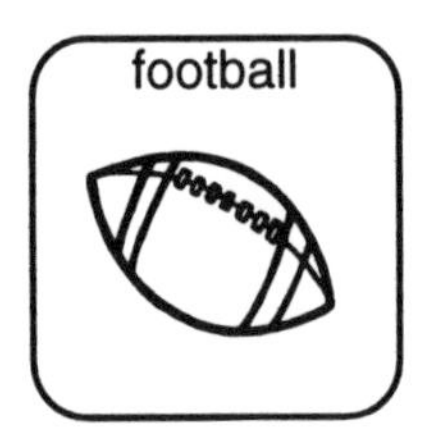

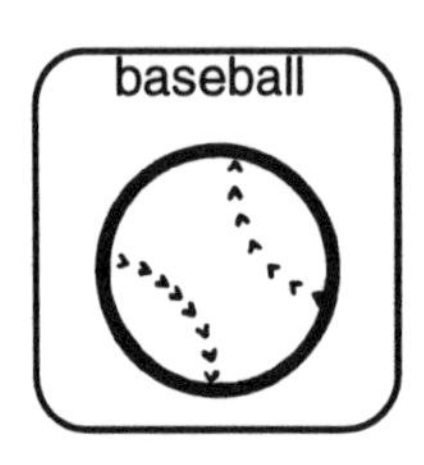

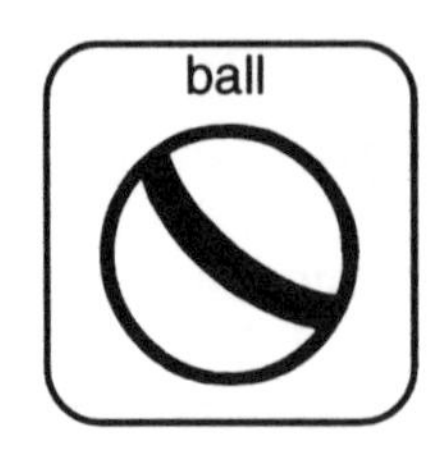

5. Which sport doesn't use a ball?

Bowling Alley
Job List

Opening Doors ______________________

____

Renting Shoes ______________________

____

Score Keeper ______________________

____

Disinfecting Shoes ______________________

____

Handling Money ______________________

____

Putting Away Bowling Balls ______________________

____

Switches Programmed For ______________________

____

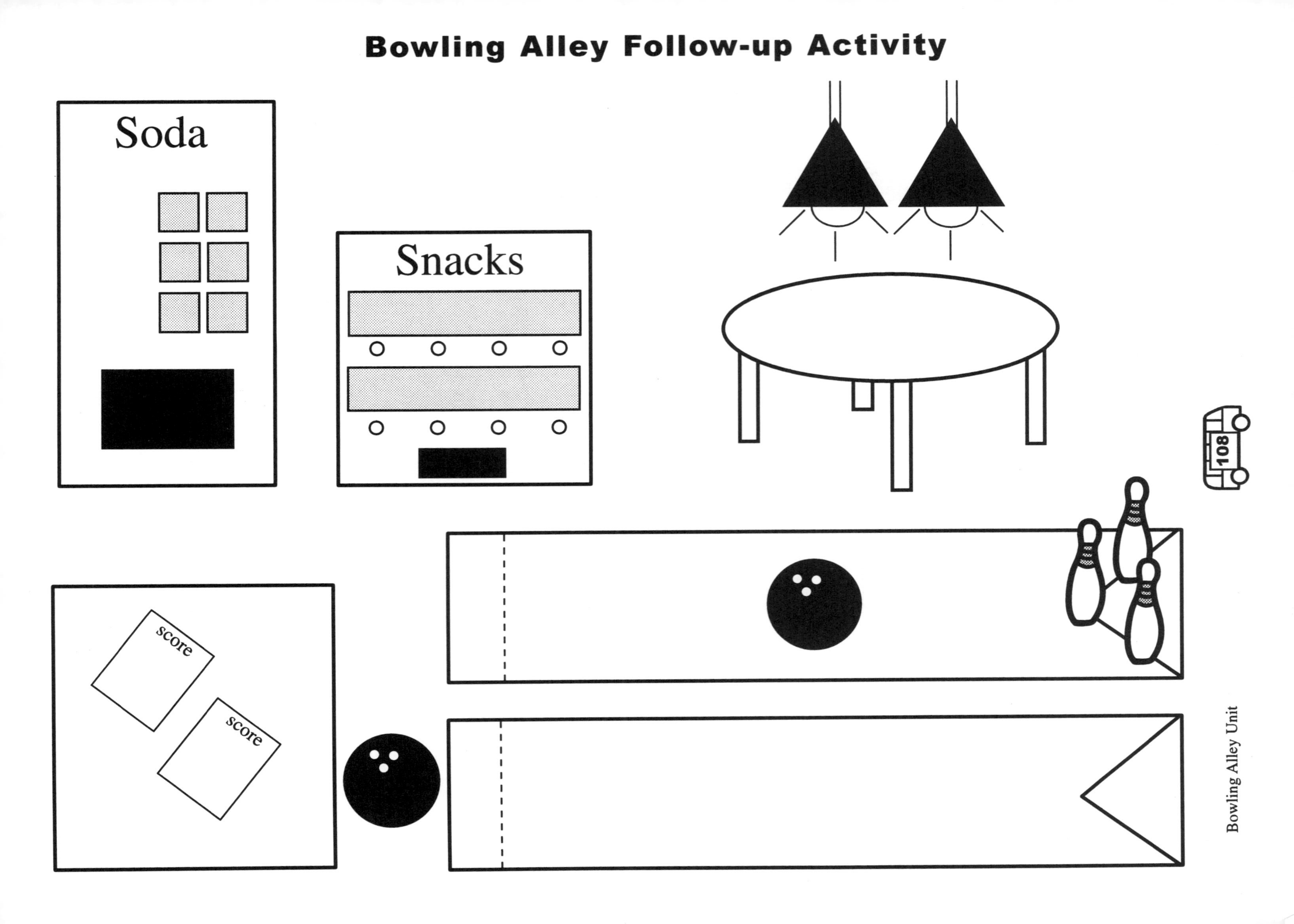
Bowling Alley Follow-up Activity
Soda
Snacks
score
score

Bowling Alley Follow-up Activity Cutouts

Directions: The following items are to be used with the Bowling Alley Follow-up Activity on page 108. Duplicate, color, and laminate both pages. Cut out items on this page. Attach a reusable adhesive (such as Fun-Tak®) to the back of each item. As you say the shape, have the student match the shape to the correct item in the correct area of the Bowling Alley.

Bowling Alley Charting Form

Name ____________________

DATE				
Big				
Little				
Circle				
Triangle				
Square				
Rectangle				
Roll				
Pin				
Ball				
Shoes				
Lane				
Spare				
Strike				
Price				
Clerk				
Open				
Close				
Push				
Pull				
Yes				
No				
Please				
Thank you				

FINE MOTOR				
Opening Door				
Closing Door				
Cutting				
Coloring				
Tying Shoes				
Vending Machine				
Grasping Ball				
Spraying Can				
Writing				
Handling Money				

VP = Verbal Prompt PP = Physical Prompt HH = Hand Over Hand + = Independent - = Incapable

Notes:

Bowling Alley
Related Materials

Books

The Magic Bowling Ball by Vivian Dubrovin. MN:EMC Corporation, 1974.

Other Sports Related Books
Franklin Plays the Game by Paulette Bourgeois and Brenda Clark. NY:Scholastic, Inc., 1995.
Clifford's Sports Day by Norman Bridwell. NY:Scholastic, Inc., 1996.
Baseball Mouse by Syd Hoff. NY:G.P. Putnam's Sons, 1969.
Soccer Game by Grace Maccarone. NY:Scholastic, Inc., 1994.
Kenny and the Little Kickers by Claudio Marzollo. NY:Scholastic, Inc., 1992.

Related Software

Where Does My Money Go? available through PCI
Plan Your Day Dictionary available through Edmark

Related Toys

Bowling ball
Bowling pins
Sample score sheets

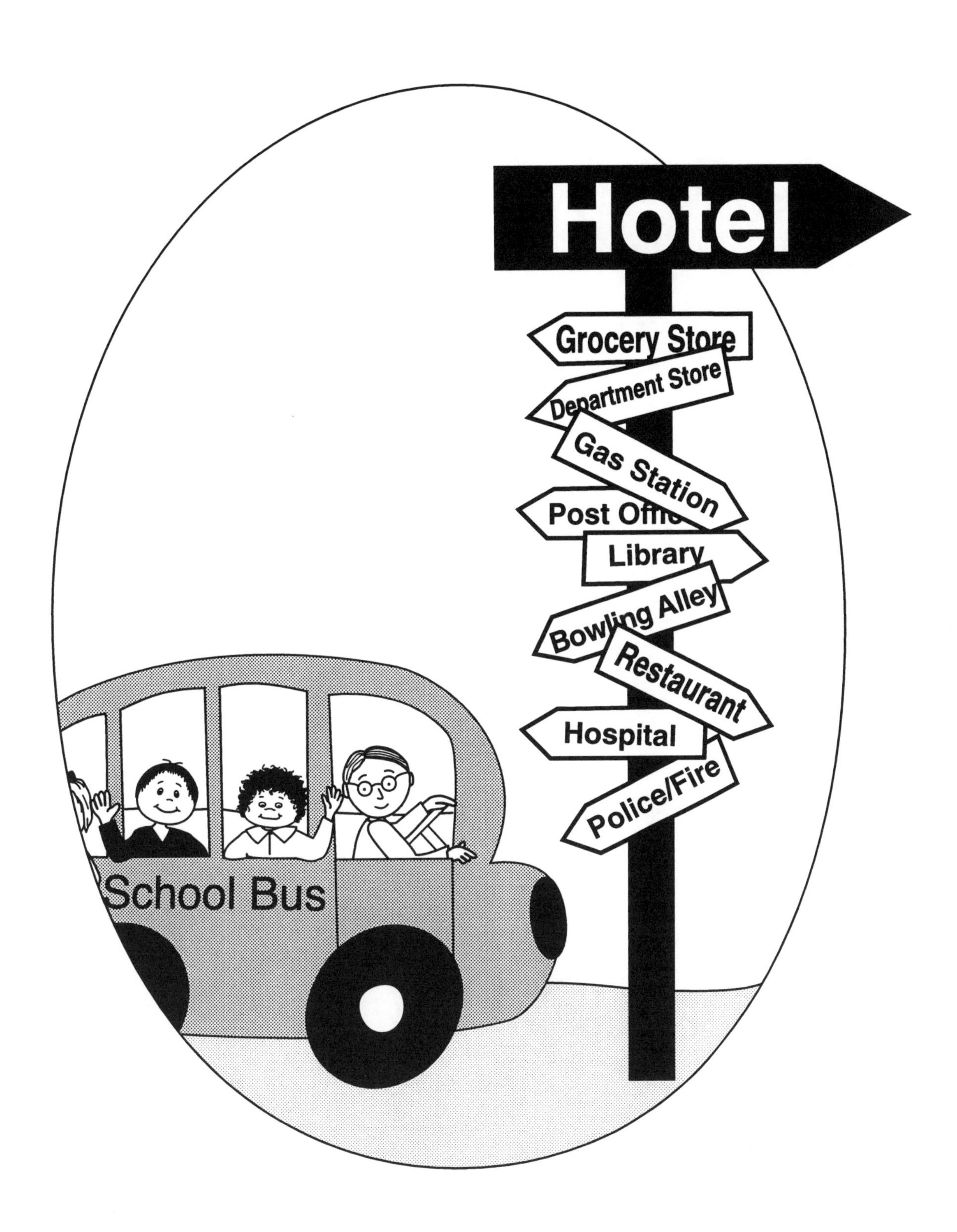
Hotel
Grocery Store
Department Store
Gas Station
Post
Library
Alley
Restaurant
Hospital
Police/Fire
School Bus

Hotel

Getting Ready To Go

1. First tell your class where you are going on your trip and practice using your communication boards.
2. Discuss the behavior you expect (you may need to model appropriate behavior and do some role playing).
3. Practice packing a small bag. Take the bag you packed on your trip.
4. Designate responsibilities (see Job List, page 123).
5. Preprogram switches/augmentative communication devices to reflect the field trip you are taking.
6. Check to make sure all permission slips have been signed.
7. Grab the communication boards and let's go!!!

Vocabulary List

color words, numbers, big, little, wet
dry, cold, up, down, middle
top, bottom, open, close, push
pull, bed, dresser, bathroom, towel
television, key, pillow, clothing, toothbrush
yes, no, please, thank you

Language Skills

categorizing
sentence structure
labeling
switch use
identifying attributes
pragmatic skills

Fine Motor Skills

opening/closing vehicle door
folding
operating laundry machines
dressing skills
cutting
measuring
brushing teeth
hanging up clothing
coloring
using a key
brushing hair

Picture Vocabulary Words

Directions: Use the picture vocabulary words to review words and symbols that are new to your students.

Hotel Activities

Level I

1. Show your students the locked door. Ask them, *"What do we need to open the door?"*
2. Show your students the hotel room. Ask them, *"What do we sleep on? Where are the pillows?"*
3. Have your students indicate yes/no to the following questions:
   "Do we put our clothes in the bathtub?" (Place bag in bathtub.)
   "Do we sleep on the dresser?" (Put a pillow on the dresser.)
   "Do we watch the cartoons on the television?" (Turn on the TV.)

Level II

1. Show your students the door to a room. Ask them, *"What do we use to unlock the door?"*
2. Have your students label items in the room. Show them the TV, pillow, bed, bathroom, and ask them, *"What is this?"*
3. Have your students practice number concepts 0-5. *"How many televisions, pillows, beds, etc., are there?"*
4. Have your students ask housekeeping for extra pillows using their communication board.
   Suggested sequence:
   "I need help. Please. 2 (number) pillows. Thank you."
5. Have your students identify and discuss the functions of various items found in the room.
   "What do we sleep on?"
   "What is found on the bed?"
   "What do we watch for fun?"

Level III

1. Have your students tell you where you plan to go and what you will find there. *"Where are we going today? What will we find there?"*
2. Have your students use their communication boards to ask the clerk how much a room will cost for one night.
   Suggested sequence:
   "I need help. Please. 1 (number) bed. How much is it? Thank you."
3. Have your students estimate how much it will cost for a hotel room for two nights. *"How much would it cost to stay two nights?"*
4. Discuss with your students the process of getting ready to spend the night at a hotel. Ask them, *"What do we do before we go to a hotel? What do we pack? Where do we go at the hotel to ask for help?"*

Hotel — Level I
Communication Board

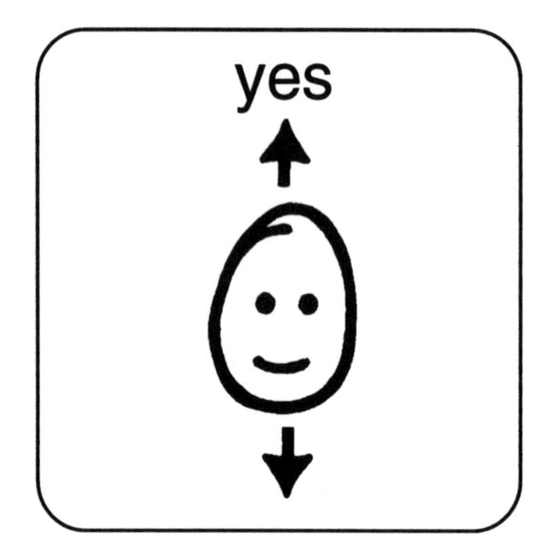

Hotel — Level II
Communication Board

0

2

3

4

5

Hotel — Level III
Communication Board

hotel

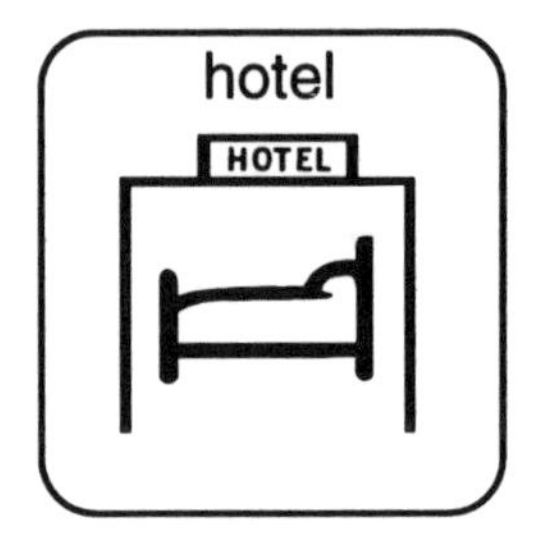

key

pillow

bed

pack

shirt

pants

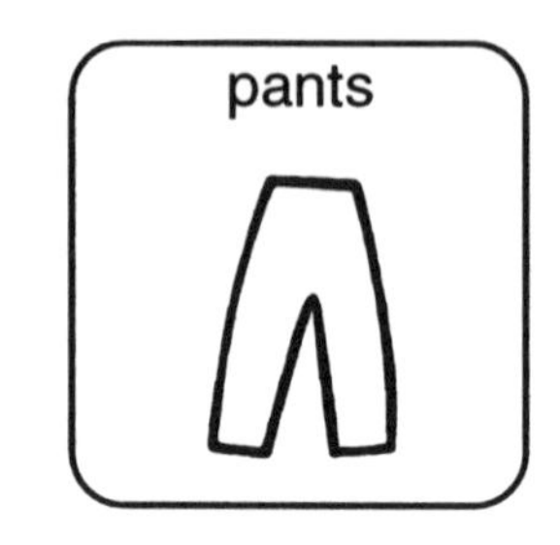

underwear

toothbrush

front desk

towel

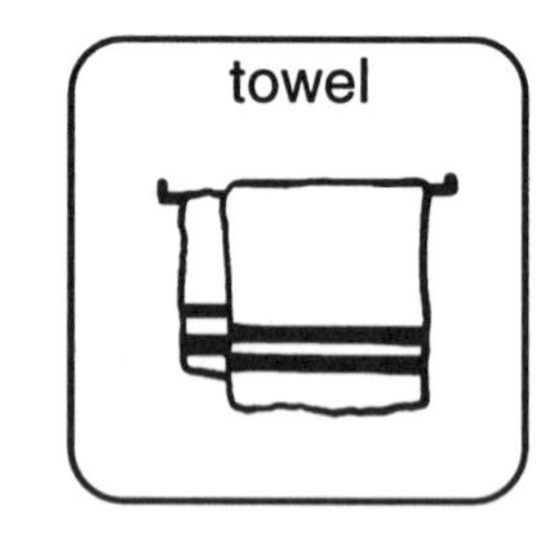

soap

How much is it?

? $

I need help

please

thank you

0	1	2	3	4	5	6	7	8	9

Hotel
Follow-up Activities

Fine Motor & Follow-up Activities

- Practice math skills using the price of a room.
- Practice making a bed.
- Practice folding towels.
- Practice folding sheets.
- Practice using keys.
- Feather painting.
- Practice using washing machine and dryer.

- Practice measurement using detergent.
- Practice daily living skills, such as brushing teeth, hair, etc.

Transition Activities for Older Students

- Vacuum floors.
- Wash bedding, towels, etc.
- Make beds.
- Fold towels and bedding.
- Dust furniture in rooms.
- Empty trash cans.
- Clean windows and mirrors.
- Load vending machines.
- Clean and stock bathrooms.

All on-site work activities will initially require supervision. If your student is high functioning, this may eventually turn into an independent work situation. Refer to introduction regarding developing work sites, page I-7.

Hotel Worksheet

Name:______________________________ Date:______________

1. What item is not found in a hotel room?

2. What do you use to open the door to the room?

3. What do you pack clothes in when traveling?

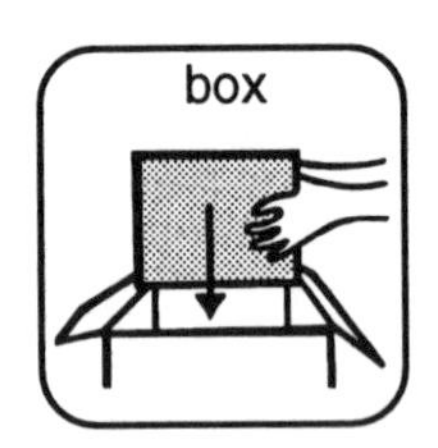

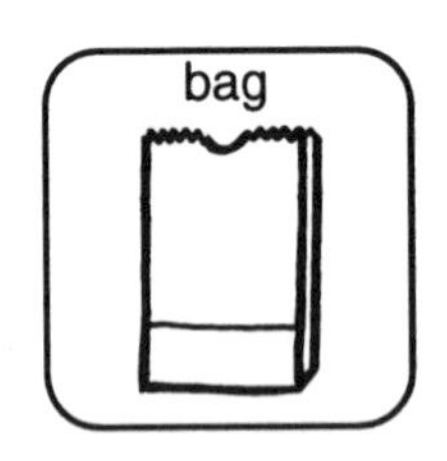

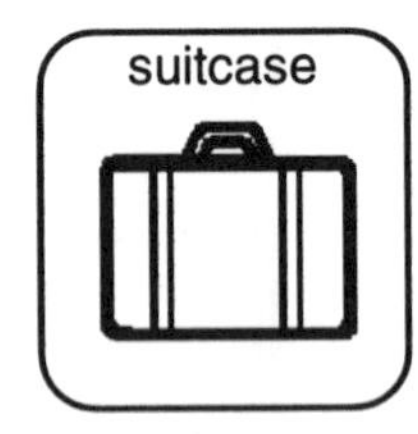

4. What would you sleep on in the hotel room?

5. What would you find in the hotel bathroom?

Hotel
Job List

Opening Doors ______________________________

____

Making Bed ______________________________

____

Unpacking Bag ______________________________

____

Folding Towels ______________________________

____

Hanging Up Clothes ______________________________

____

Switches Programmed For ______________________________

____

Hotel Follow-up Activity

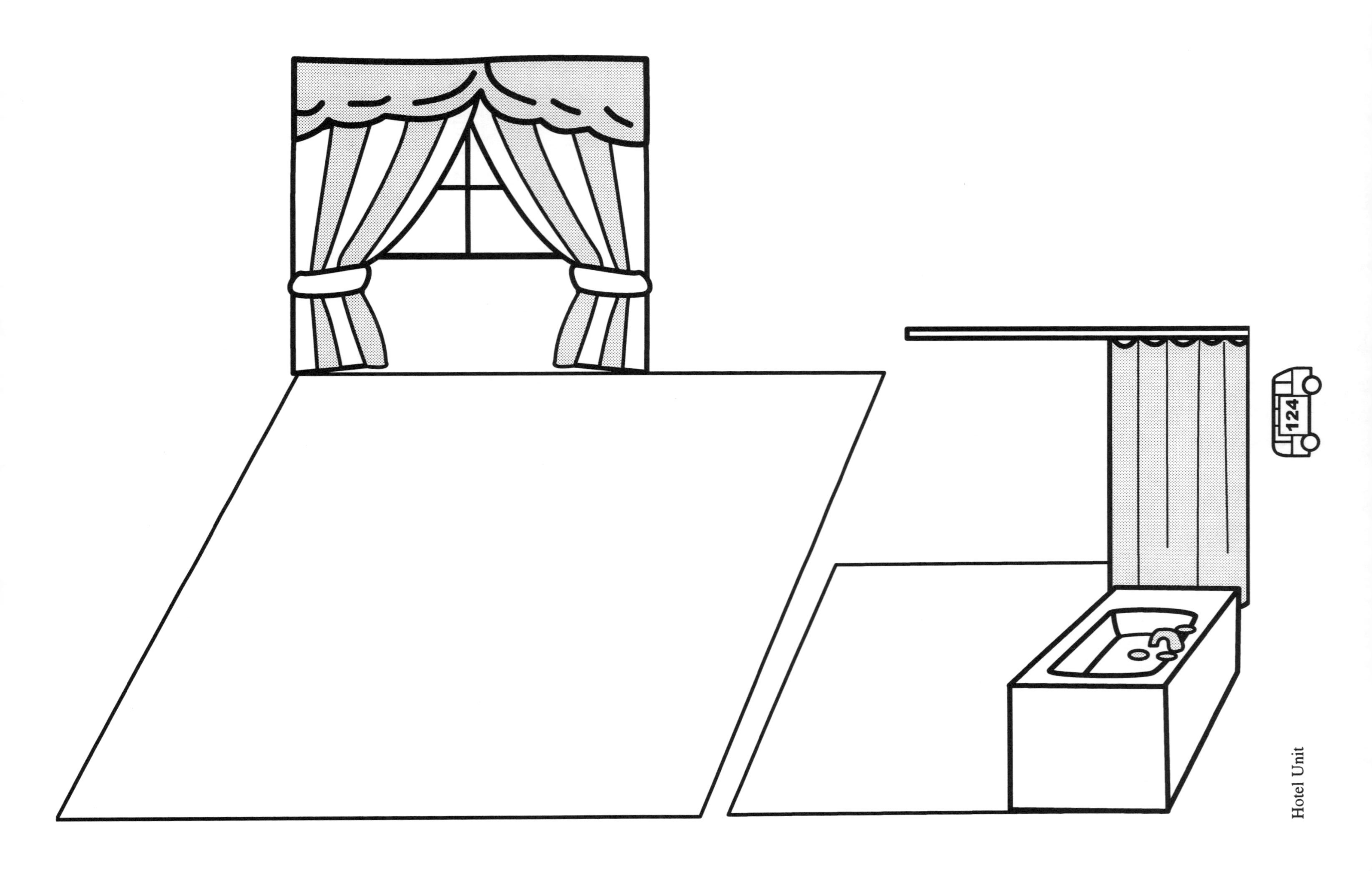

Hotel Follow-up Activity Cutouts

Directions: The following items are to be used with the Hotel Follow-up Activity, page 124. Duplicate both pages. Color, cut out, and laminate items on this page. Attach a reusable adhesive (such as Fun-Tak®) to the back of each item. In addition, color, and laminate the Hotel Follow-up Activity page. As you say the name of the item, have the student place it in the correct room of the hotel.

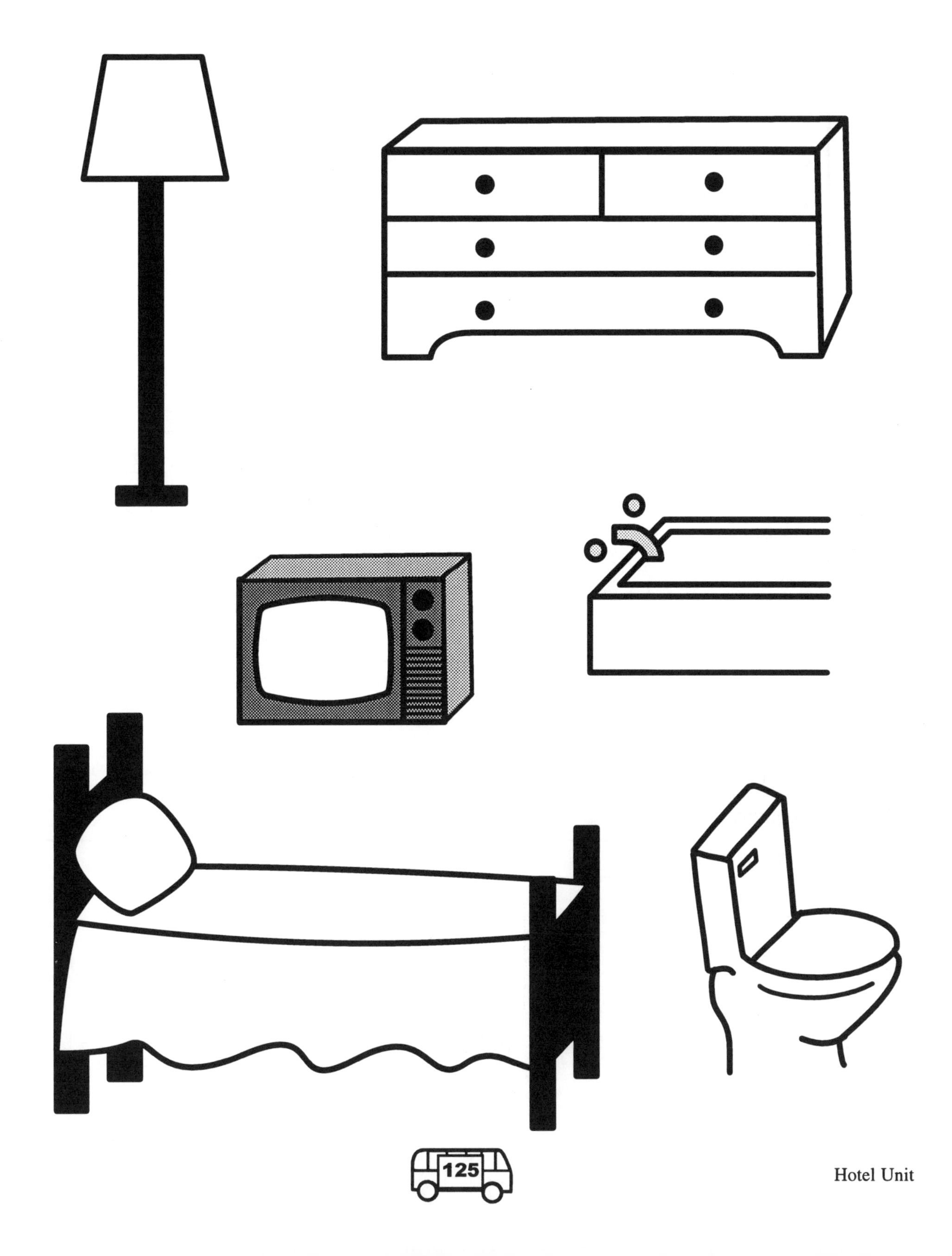

Hotel Charting Form

Name ______________________

DATE				
Big				
Little				
Wet				
Dry				
Cold				
Up				
Down				
Middle				
Top				
Bottom				
Open				
Close				
Push				
Pull				
Bed				
Dresser				
Bathroom				
Towel				
Television				
Key				
Pillow				
Clothing				
Toothbrush				
Yes				
No				
Please				
Thank you				

FINE MOTOR				
Opening Door				
Closing Door				
Cutting				
Coloring				
Folding				
Measuring				
Using Key				
Using Washer				
Using Dryer				
Brushing Teeth				

VP = Verbal Prompt PP = Physical Prompt HH = Hand Over Hand + = Independent - = Incapable

Notes:

Hotel
Related Materials

Books

Buzby to the Rescue by Julia Hoban. USA:Harper Collins, 1993.
Funny Bunnies by Robert Quackenbush. NY:Clarion Books, 1984.
The Bag I'm Taking to Grandma's by Shirley Nietzel. NY:Greenwillow Books, 1995.
Do You See a Mouse? by Bernard Waber. MA:Houghton Mifflin Co., 1995.

Related Software

Keeping House Dictionary available through Edmark

Related Toys

Toy broom
Toy vacuum
Toy laundry center
Toy ironing board

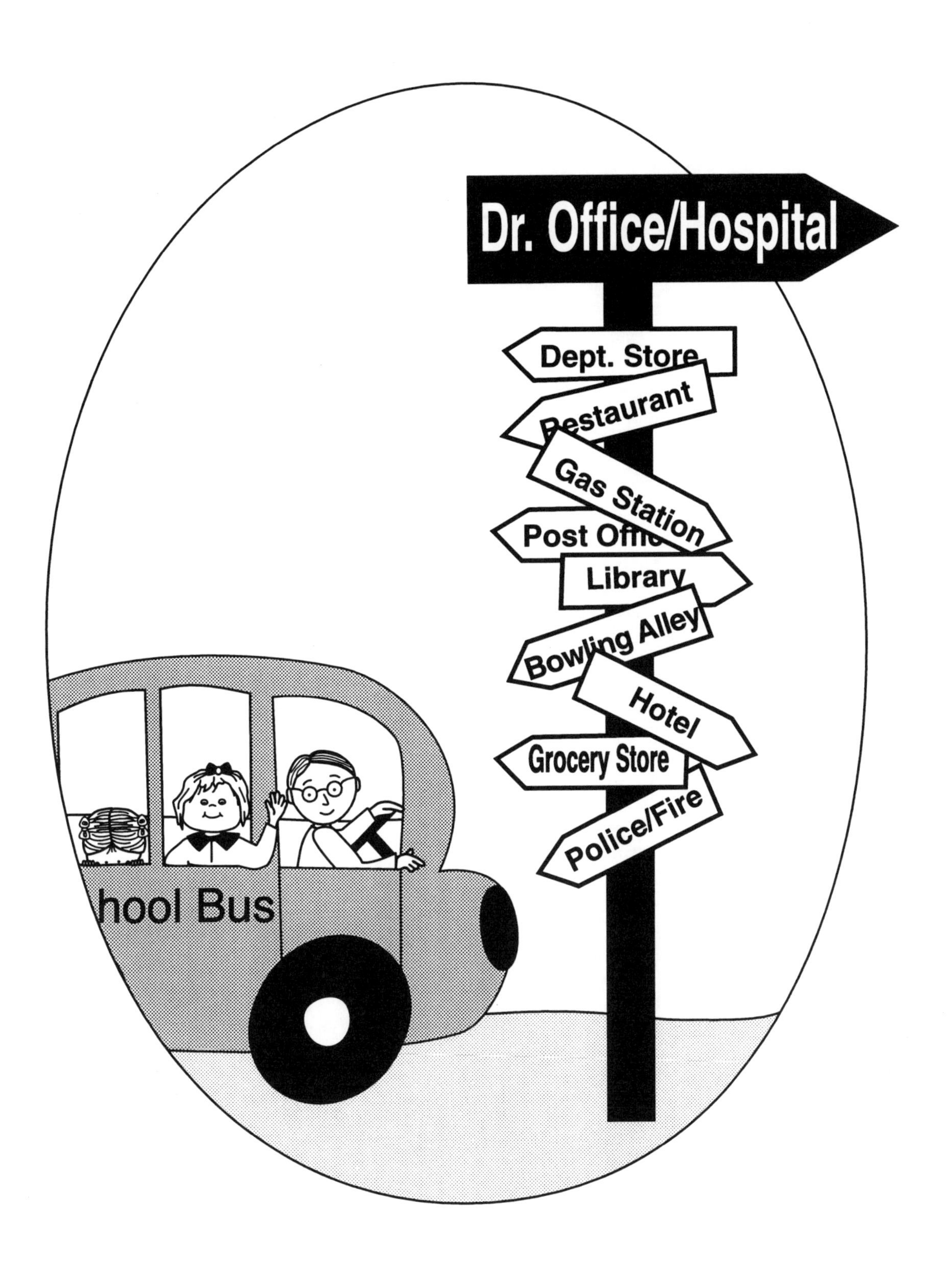
Dr. Office/Hospital
Dept. Store
Restaurant
Gas Station
Post Office
Library
Bowling Alley
Hotel
Grocery Store
Police/Fire
hool Bus

Dr. Office/Hospital

Getting Ready To Go

1. First tell your class where you are going on your trip and practice using your communication boards.
2. Discuss the behavior you expect (you may need to model appropriate behavior and do some role playing).
3. Discuss personal health and hygiene.
4. Bring a doll or stuffed animal for students to practice on.
5. Preprogram switches/augmentative communication devices to reflect the field trip you are taking.
6. Check to make sure all permission slips have been signed.
7. Grab the communication boards and let's go!!!

Vocabulary List

color words	numbers	hurt	sick	Band-Aid
blood pressure	medicine	X ray	shot	
stethoscope				
thermometer	otoscope	scale	open	close
push	pull	yes	no	please
thank you				

Language Skills

categorizing	labeling	identifying attributes
sentence structure	switch use	pragmatic skills

Fine Motor Skills

opening/closing doors	opening Band-Aids	wrapping
operating tape recorder	opening/closing fasteners	dressing
squeezing blood pressure cuff	cutting	coloring
painting		

Picture Vocabulary Words

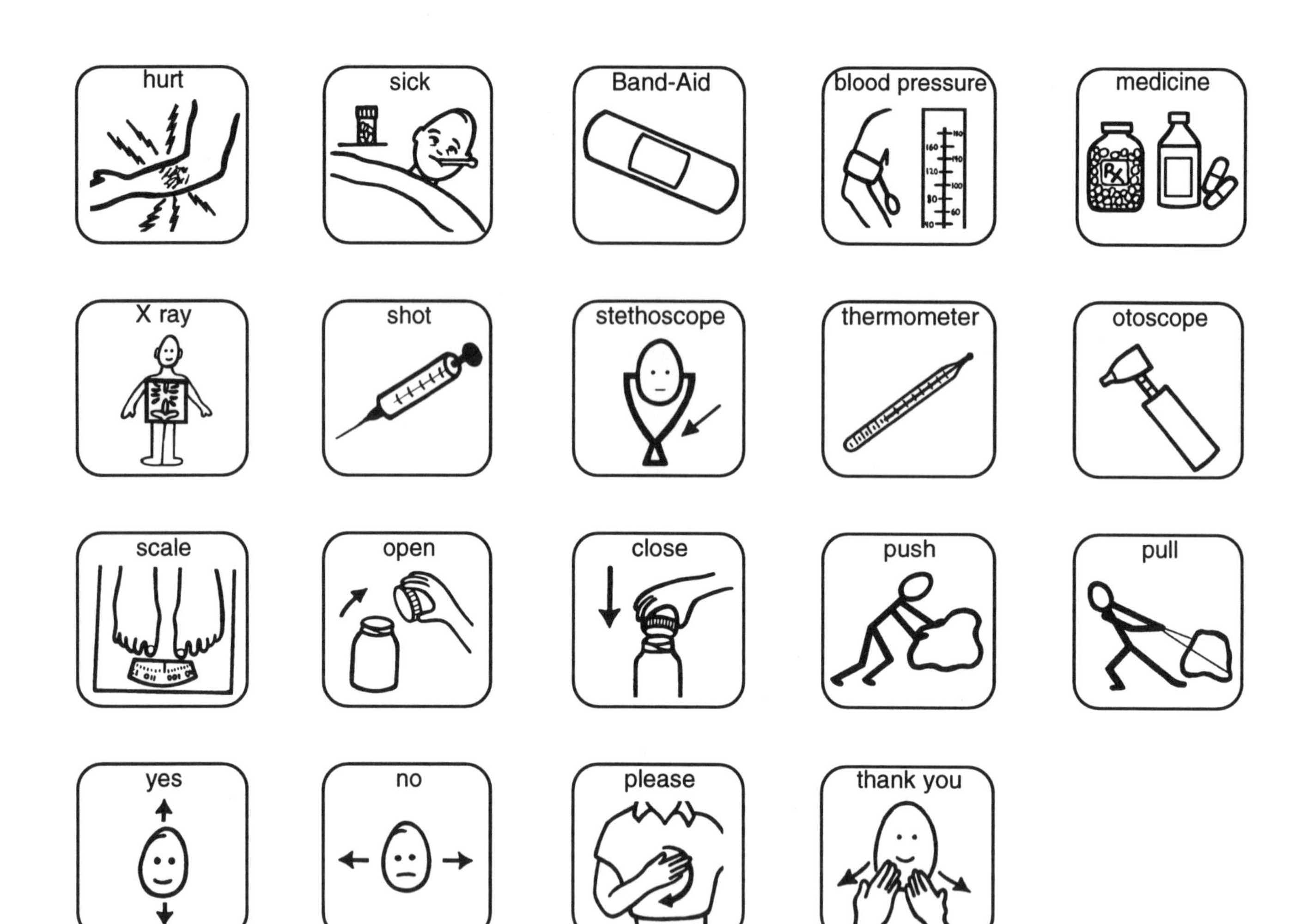

Directions: Use the picture vocabulary words to review words and symbols that are new to your students.

Dr. Office/Hospital
Activities

Level I

1. Ask your students to use their communication boards to tell you who works at a hospital/clinic. *"Who works at the hospital?"*
2. Show your students various medical equipment (bandages, medicine bottles, tongue depressors) and have them use their communication boards to indicate when you would use these items. *"When would we use these? Who would give them to us?"*
3. Have your students indicate yes/no to the following questions:
   "Are these toys?" (Show him/her medical equipment.)
   "Do we wear these when we are hurt?" (Show him/her bandages.)
   "Do we put the thermometer in our nose?" (Show him/her a thermometer.)

Level II

1. Have your students label items that you point to in the room. Show them a stethoscope, blood pressure cuff, Band-Aid and ask them, *"What is this?"*
2. Have your students practice number concepts 0-5 using items found in the room. *"How many tongue depressors, Band-Aids, Q-tips, etc., am I holding up?"*
3. Have your students use their communication boards to answer the following questions relating to the functions of various items:
   "What do we use to listen to our heart?"
   "What feels tight on your arm when the nurse pumps it up?"
   "What do we put on a cut?"
4. Have your students demonstrate the appropriate use of some of the items found in the room. Have them use these items on each other or on a doll/stuffed animal they have brought with them. Suggested items include Band Aids, stethoscope, blood pressure cuff, and tongue depressors.

Level III

1. Have your students tell you where you plan to go and what you will find there. *"Where are we going today? What will we find there?"*
2. Have your students estimate how much they weigh after weighing yourself or another student. *"How much do you think you weigh?"*
3. Have your students use their communication boards to answer the following questions relating to the functions of various items:
   "What do we use to listen to our heart?"
   "What feels tight on your arm when the nurse pumps it up?"
   "What do we put on a cut?"
   "What does the doctor use to look in our ears?"
   "What does the doctor give us when we are sick to make us feel better?"
   "What do we use to take our temperature?"
   "What does the doctor use to look at our bones?"
   "What do we wear when the doctor examines us?"

Dr. Office/Hospital — Level I Communication Board

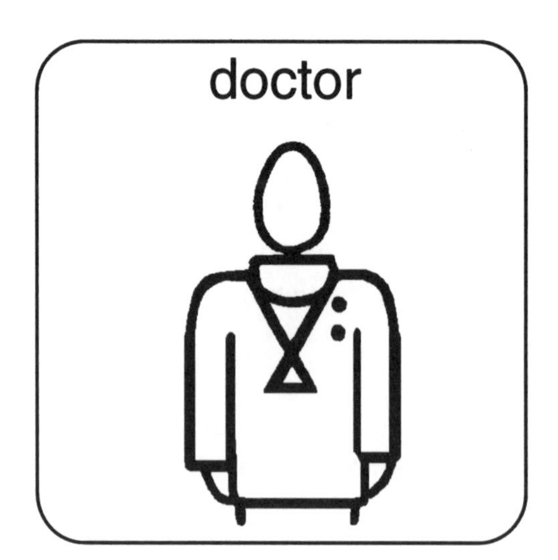

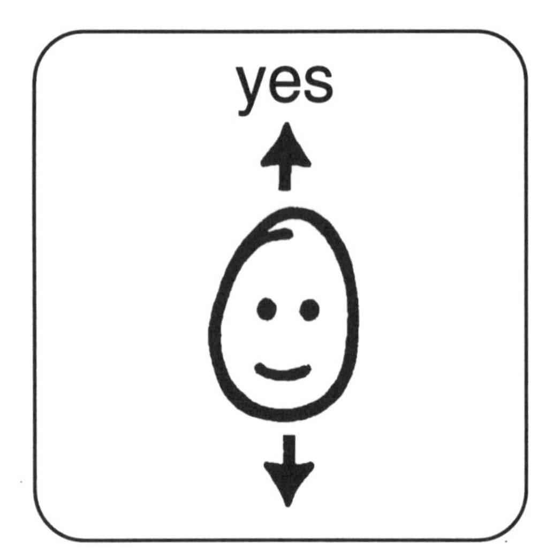

Dr. Office/Hospital — Level II Communication Board

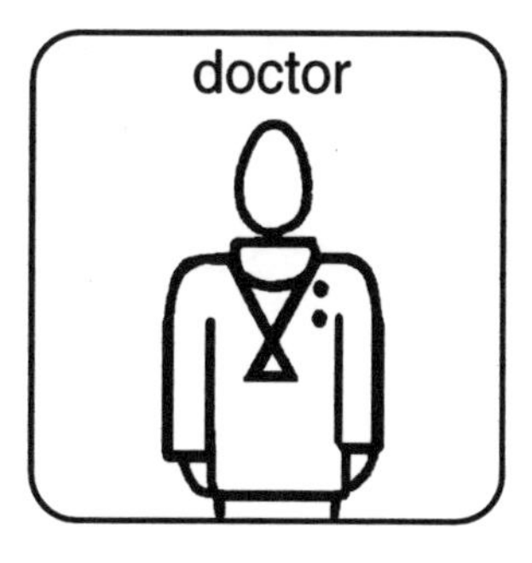

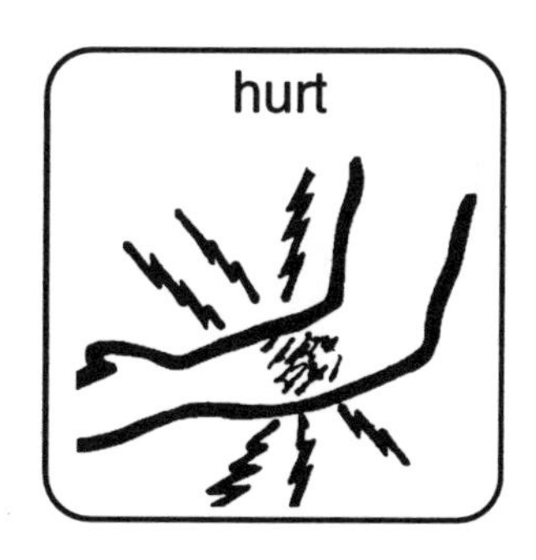

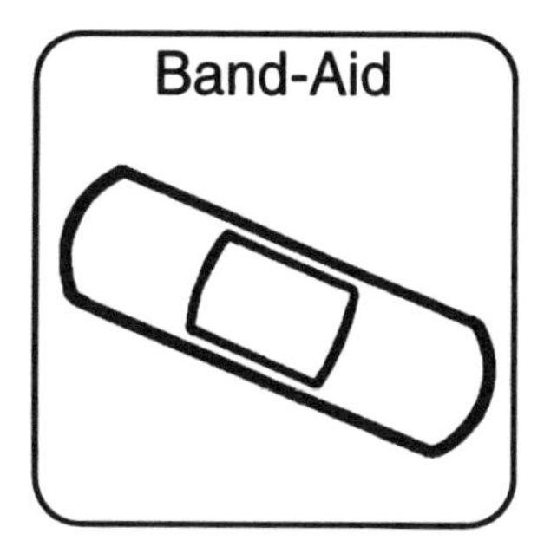

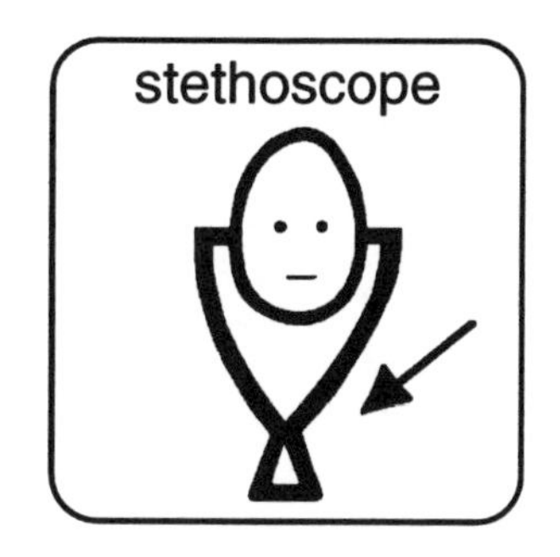

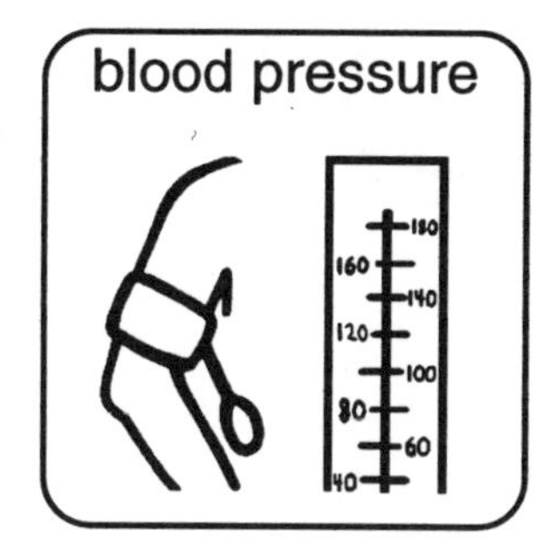

0 1 2 3 4 5

Dr. Office/Hospital — Level III Communication Board

hospital

doctor
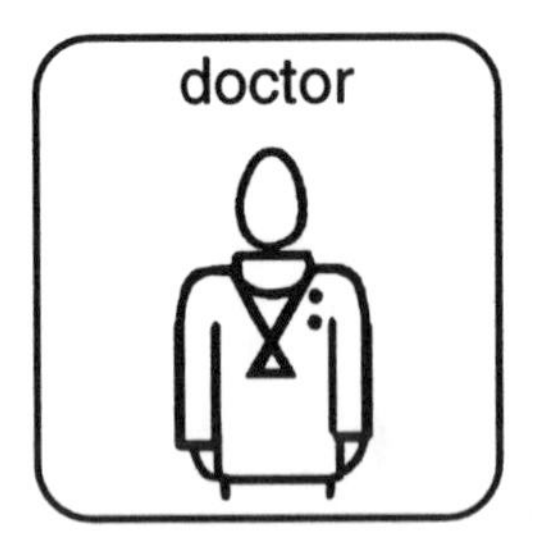

hurt
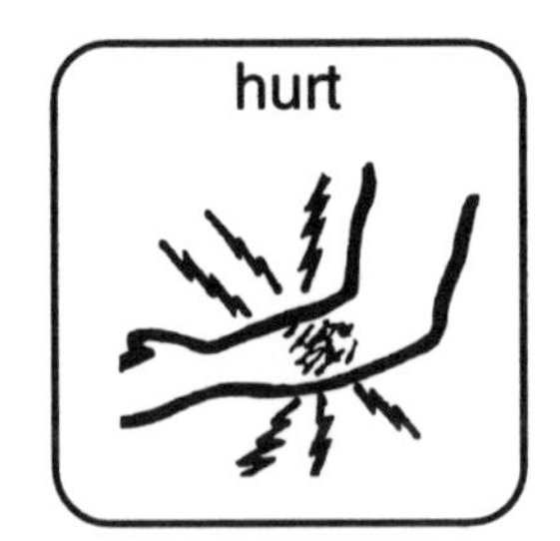

sick

hospital gown

blood pressure
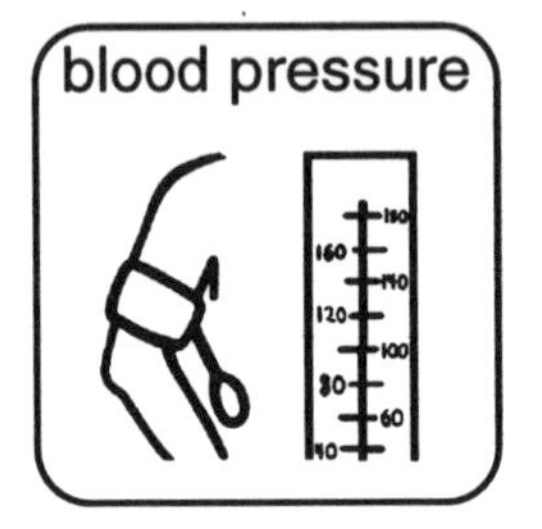

stethoscope

Band-Aid
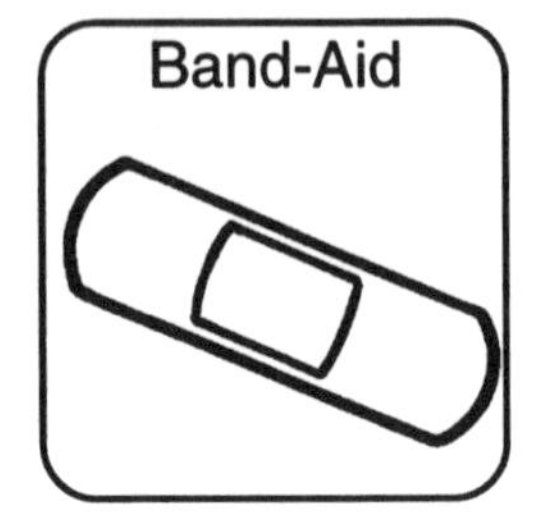

scale
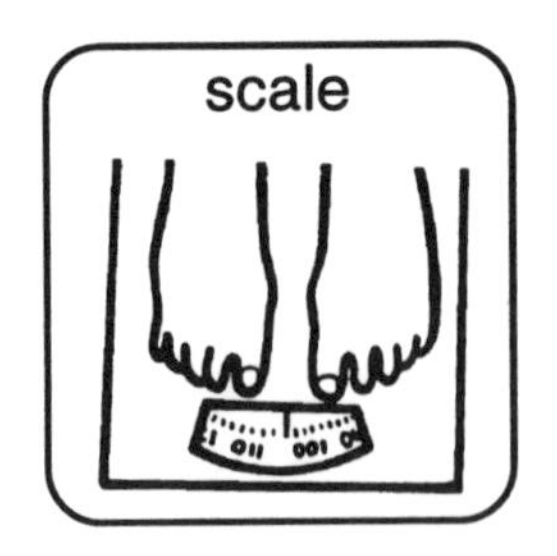

medicine
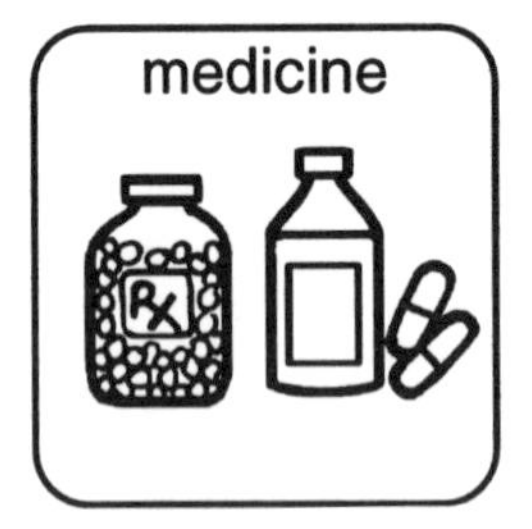

X ray
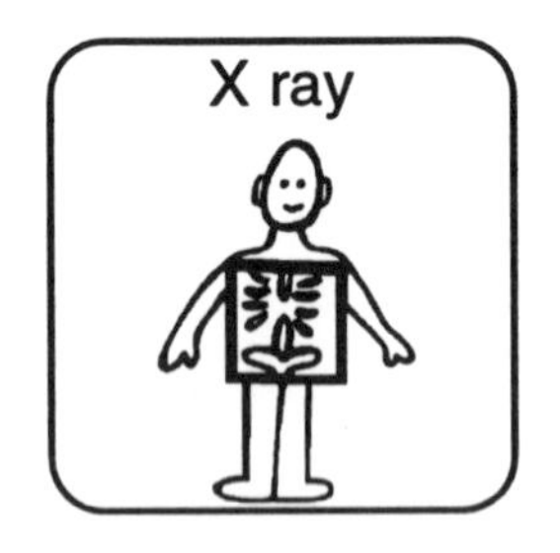

shot
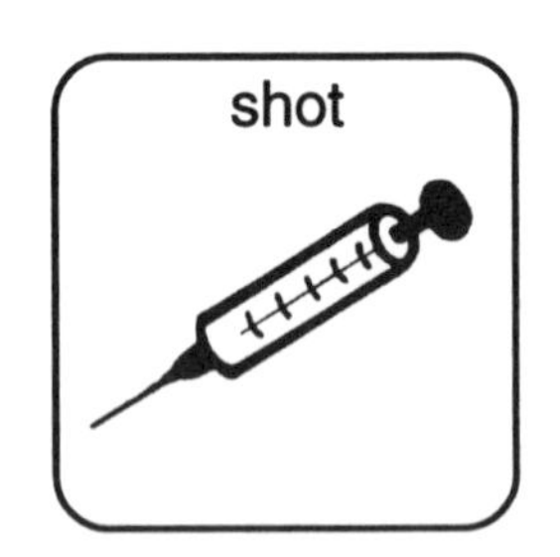

otoscope
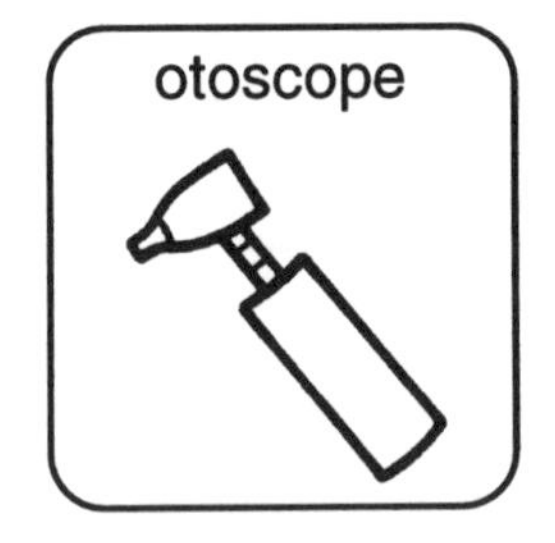

thermometer
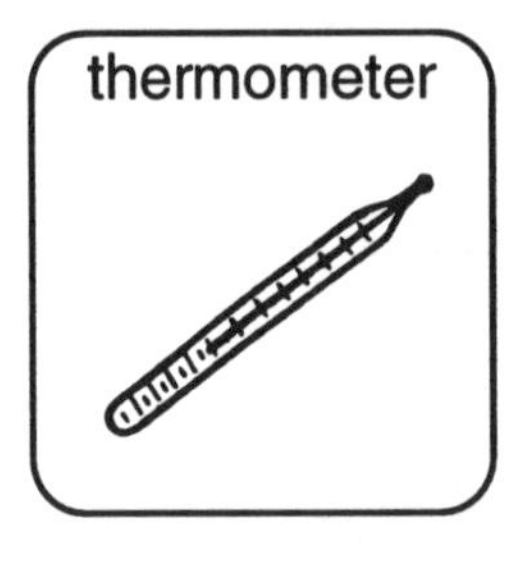

please

thank you

0	1	2	3	4	5	6	7	8	9

Dr. Office/Hospital
Follow-up Activities

Fine Motor & Follow-up Activities

Use students and/or stuffed animals to role-play using basic or toy medical equipment.

Practice opening and putting on Band-Aids. Compile a basic first-aid kit for school and home.

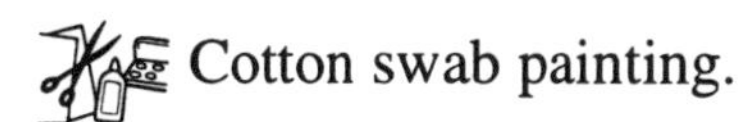
Cotton swab painting.

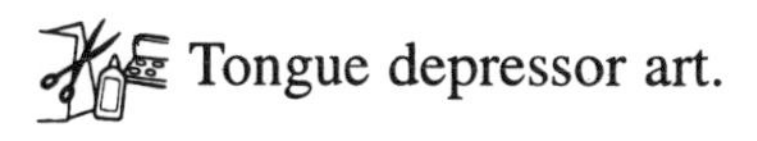
Tongue depressor art.

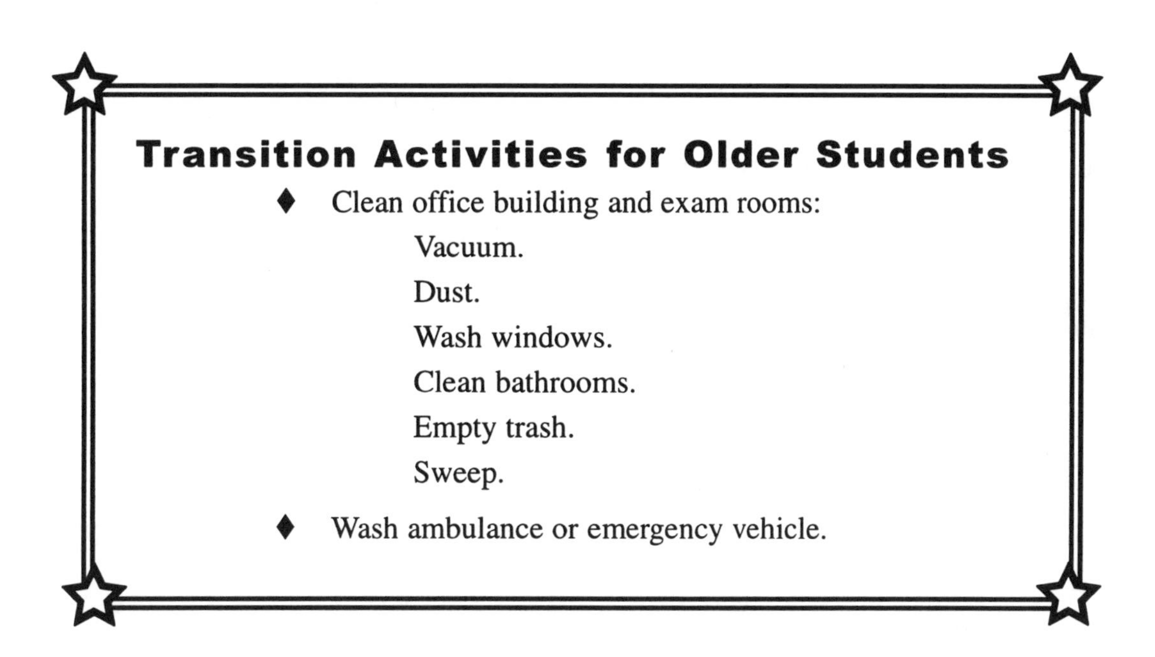

Transition Activities for Older Students

- Clean office building and exam rooms:
  - Vacuum.
  - Dust.
  - Wash windows.
  - Clean bathrooms.
  - Empty trash.
  - Sweep.
- Wash ambulance or emergency vehicle.

All on-site work activities will initially require supervision. If your student is high functioning, this may eventually turn into an independent work situation. Refer to introduction regarding developing work sites, page I-7.

Dr. Office/Hospital Worksheet

Name:______________________________ Date:______________

1. Where do you go when you are hurt?

2. What is used to take your temperature?

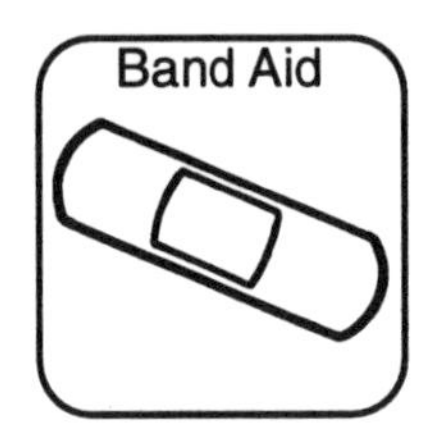

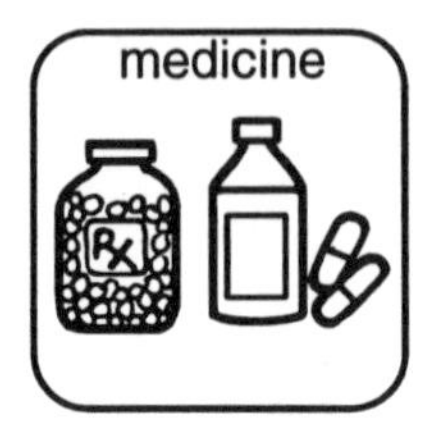

3. Who examines you at the hospital?

4. What do you put on a cut?

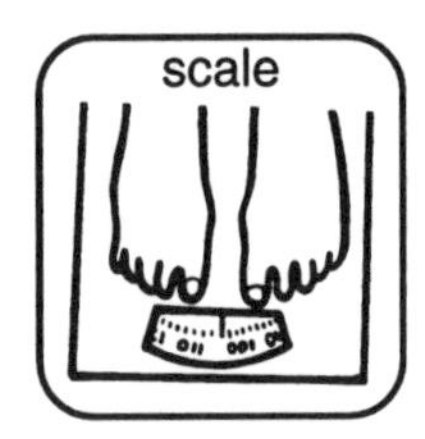

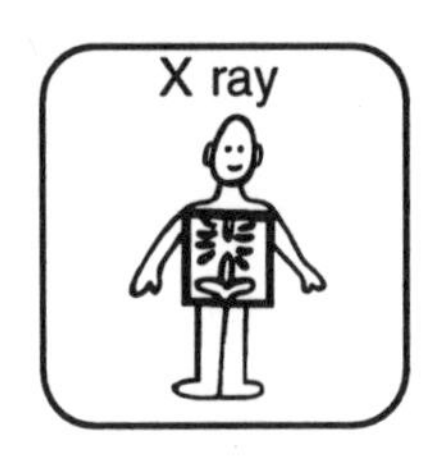

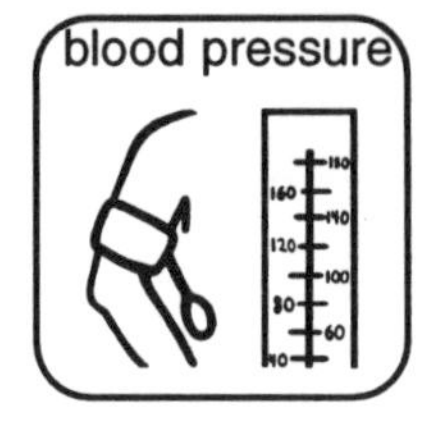

5. What tells how much you weigh?

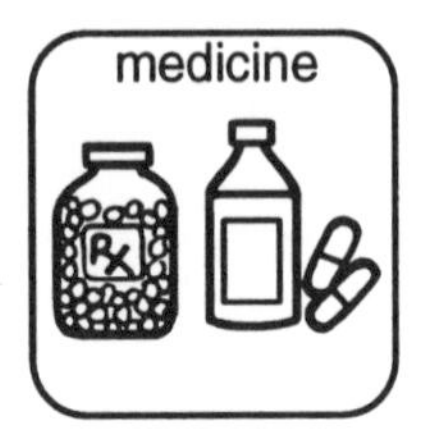

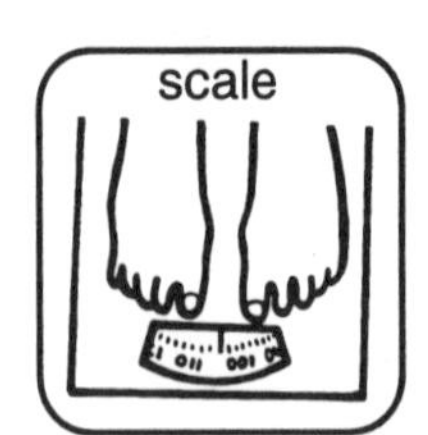

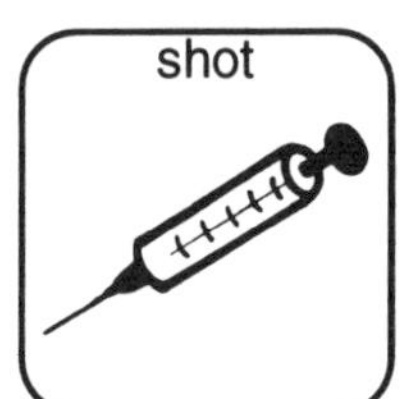

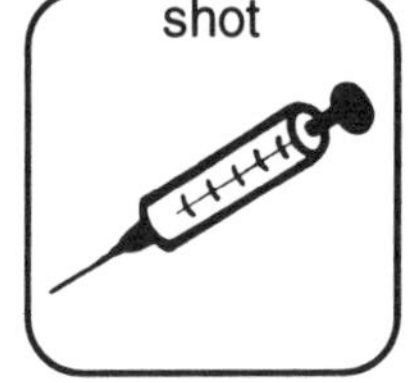

Dr. Office/Hospital Follow-up Activity

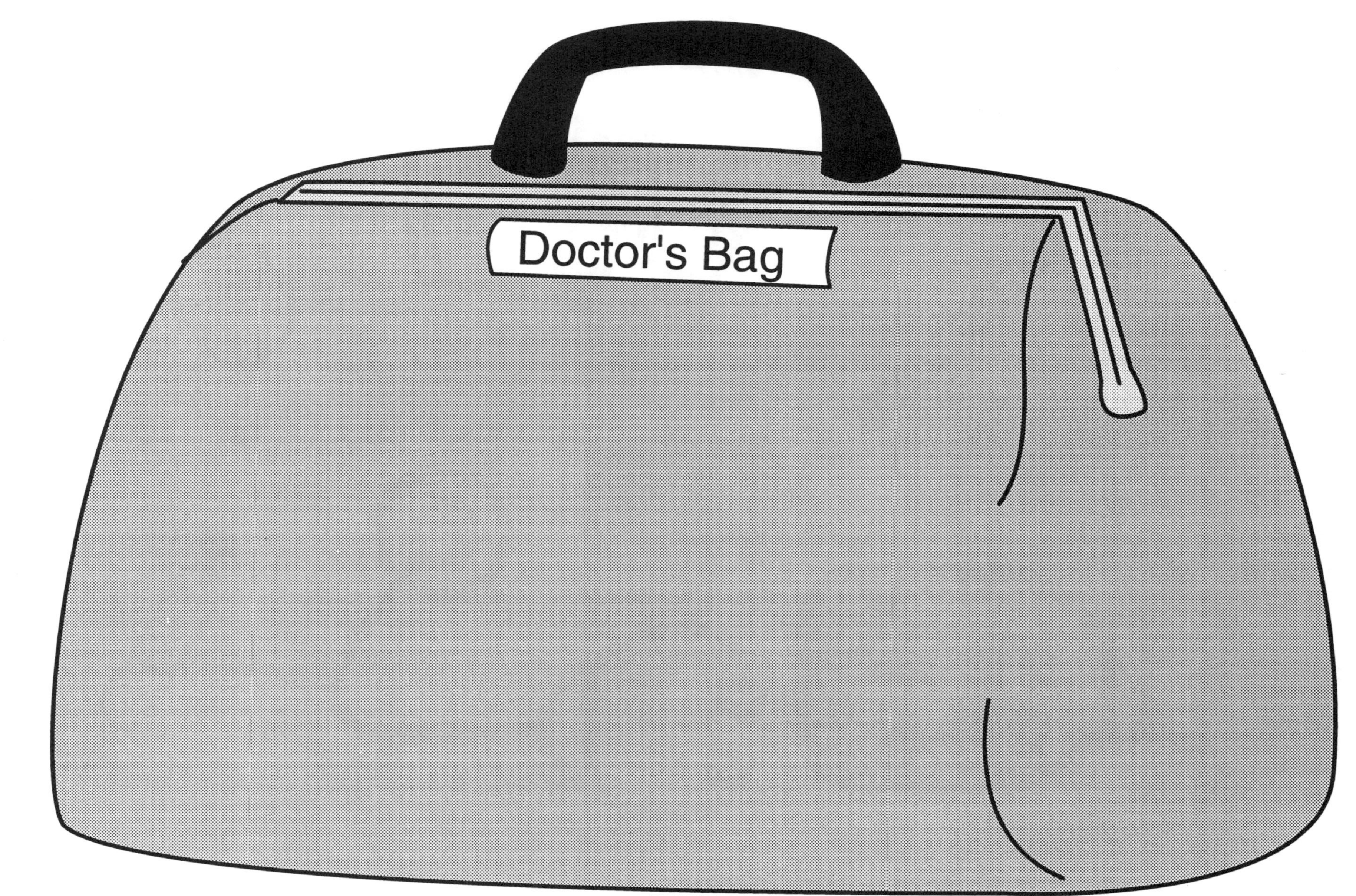

Dr. Office/Hospital Follow-up Activity Cutouts

Directions: The following items are to be used with the Dr. Office/Hospital Follow-up Activity, page 139. Duplicate both pages. Color, cut out, and laminate items on this page. Attach a reusable adhesive (such as Fun-Tak®) to the back of each item. In addition, color, and laminate the Dr. Office/Hospital Follow-up Activity page. As you say the name of the item, have the student locate the item and place it in the Doctors's Bag.

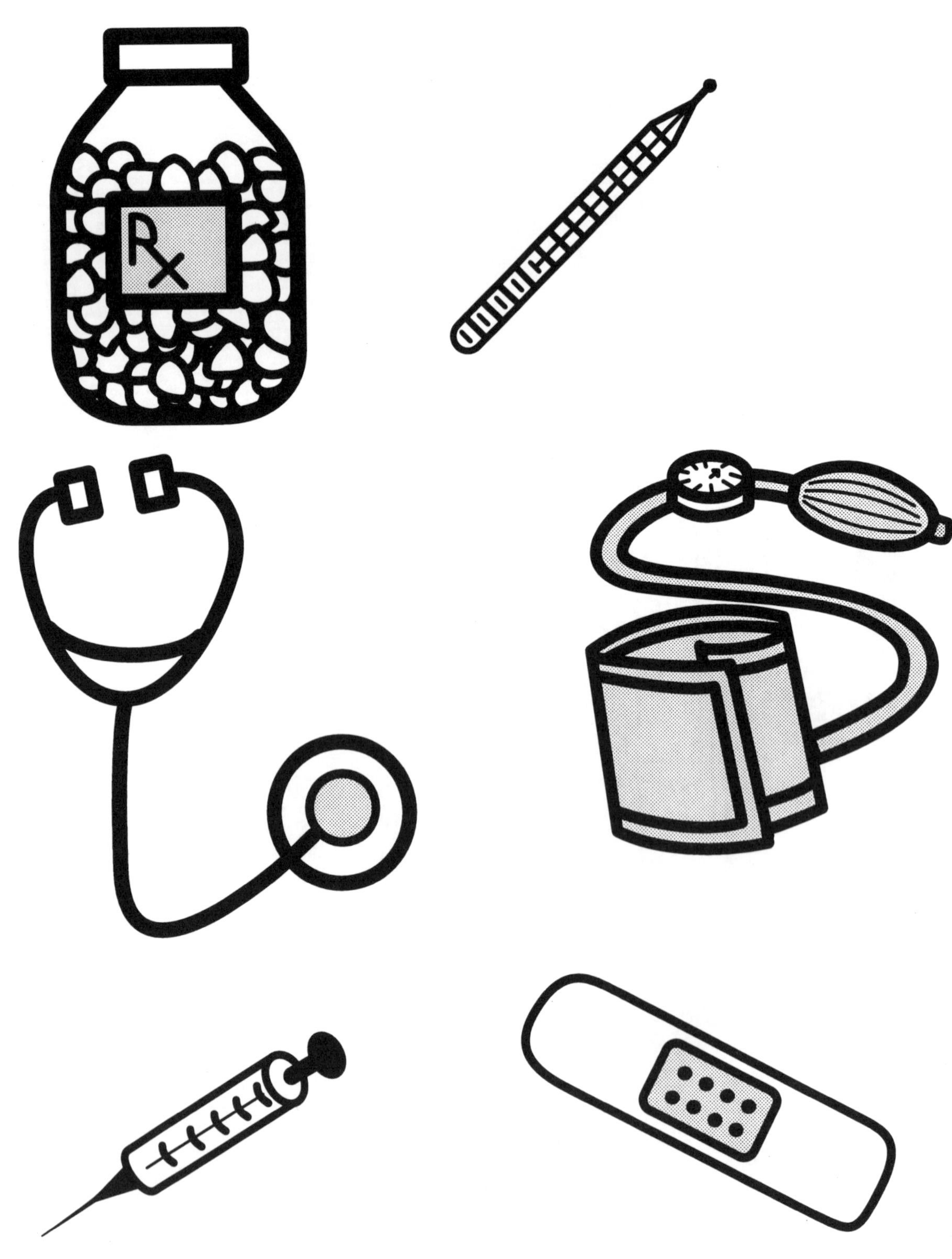

Dr. Office/Hospital Charting Form

Name ____________________

DATE				
Hurt				
Sick				
Band-Aid				
Blood Pressure				
Medicine				
X ray				
Shot				
Stethoscope				
Thermometer				
Otoscope				
Scale				
Open				
Close				
Push				
Pull				
Yes				
No				
Please				
Thank you				

FINE MOTOR				
Opening Door				
Closing Door				
Opening Band Aids				
Wrapping				
Dressing				
Snaps				
Buttons				
Zippers				
Squeezing				
Cutting				
Coloring				
Painting				

VP = Verbal Prompt PP = Physical Prompt HH = Hand Over Hand + = Independent - = Incapable

Notes:

Dr. Office/Hospital

Related Materials

Books

The Hospital Book by James Howe. NY:Crown Publishers, 1981.
Elizabeth Gets Well by Alfons Weber, MD. NY: Thomas Y. Crowell, 1970.
Come to Work with Us in a Hospital by Jean and Ned Wilkinson. WI:Sextant Systems, Inc., 1970.
Curious George Goes to the Hospital by Margret and H.A. Rey. MA:Houghton Mifflin Co, 1966.
Going to the Doctor by Fred Rogers. Canada: General Publishing Co. Limited, 1986.
A Visit to the Sesame Street Hospital by Deborah Hautiz. NY:Random House, Inc., 1985.

Related Software

Community Exploration available through Edmark
Fun Around Town through SoftWareHouse
My Town available through Edmark

Related Toys

Toy doctor kit
Dress-up clothes

Police/Fire
Grocery Store
Department Store
Restaurant
Post
Library
Alley
Hotel
Hospital
Gas Station
School Bus

Police/Fire Station  

Getting Ready To Go

1. First tell your class where you are going on your trip and practice using your communication boards.
2. Discuss the behavior you expect (you may need to model appropriate behavior and do some role playing).
3. Discuss vehicle safety.
4. Discuss fire safety.
5. Preprogram switches/augmentative communication devices to reflect the field trip you are taking.
6. Check to make sure all permission slips have been signed.
7. Grab the communication boards and let's go!!!

Vocabulary List

color words	numbers	big	little	wet
dry	up	fire truck	police car	firefighter
police officer	siren	ladder	smoke detector	open
close	push	pull	yes	no
please	thank you			

Language Skills

categorizing	labeling	identifying attributes
sentence structure	switch use	pragmatic skills

Fine Motor Skills

opening/closing doors	changing batteries	cutting
using keys	coloring	painting
fastening seat belts		

Picture Vocabulary Words

Directions: Use the picture vocabulary words to review words and symbols that are new to your students.

Police/Fire Station
Activities

Level I

1. Discuss with your students the duties of the firefighter and police officer. Have your students use their communication boards to indicate the right person. *"Who puts out fires? Who helps us obey the law?"*
2. Show your students the vehicles associated with each job. Show them the police car and ask, *"Who drives this car?"* Show them the fire truck and ask them, *"Who drives this truck?"*
3. Have your students indicate yes/no to the following questions:
   "Can we ever play with matches?" (Show them matches and discuss fire safety.)
   "Will a police officer help us if we are lost?" (Discuss personal safety.)

Level II

1. Have your students use their communication boards to answer the following questions:
   "Who drives a big red truck?"
   "Who works at the jail?"
   "What do we wear when we are in a vehicle?"
   "Who puts out a fire?"
   "What does the firefighter spray water on?"
   "What can happen if cars don't follow the laws?"
   "What do we call it when you take something that doesn't belong to you?"
   "What does a police officer drive?"
   "What does a firefighter drive?"
2. Have your students practice number concepts 0-5. *"How many tires are on the police car? How many boots do you see? How many hats do you see?"*
3. Have your students practice their manners by saying *"Thank you"* to the police officers and fire- fighters after the tour.

Level III

1. Have your students tell you where you plan to go and what you will find there. *"Where are we going today? What will we find there?"*
2. Discuss with your students reasons you would need the help of a firefighter or police officer.
3. Have your students label the items and people found at the police station and fire station. Show them jail, camera, police car, fire truck, ladder, and ask them, *"What is this?"*
4. Ask the police department if they could take the fingerprints and pictures of your students so that their parents can have these records for safety reasons.
5. Have your students use their communication boards to answer the following questions:
   "What can happen if cars don't follow the laws?"
   "What do we call it when you take something that doesn't belong to you?"
   "What do we wear when we are in a vehicle?"

Police/Fire Station — Level I
Communication Board

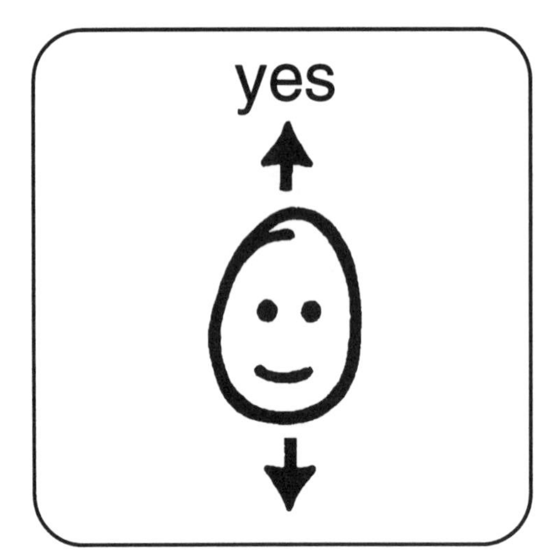

Police/Fire Station — Level II
Communication Board

0 1 2 3 4 5

Police/Fire Station — Level III
Communication Board

0	1	2	3	4	5	6	7	8	9

Police/Fire Station
Follow-up Activities

Fine Motor & Follow-up Activities

Discuss fire safety.

Discuss laws and traffic safety.

Practice understanding of basic survival signs.

Thumbprint art.

Role-play firefighter and police officer duties using costumes and props (unlocking toy handcuffs).

Practice changing batteries in smoke detectors.

Tape record basic safety messages to keep by the phone for nonverbal students to use in case of an emergency. Practice dialing emergency numbers and using the prerecorded message. (Name, address, we need help.)

Transition Activities for Older Students

- Clean the fire house and police station:
  - Dust desks.
  - Vacuum floors.
  - Clean bathrooms.
  - Wash windows.
  - Sweep floors.
- Wash vehicles.
- Load vending machines.

All on-site work activities will initially require supervision. If your student is high functioning, this may eventually turn into an independent work situation. Refer to introduction regarding developing work sites, page I-7.

Police/Fire Station Worksheet

Name:______________________________ Date:____________

1. What does the firefighter use to put water on a fire?

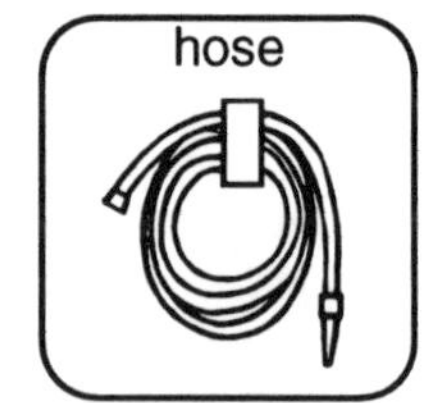

2. What item can you never play with?

3. Who enforces our laws?

4. Who could help you if you were lost?

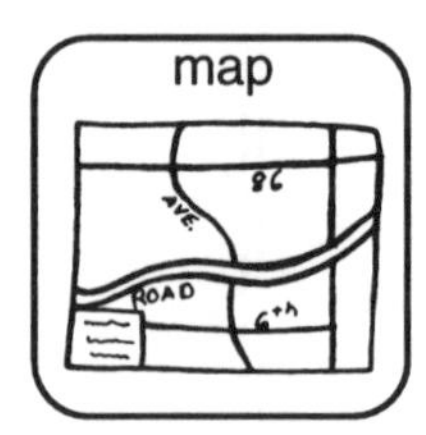

5. What does a police officer carry?

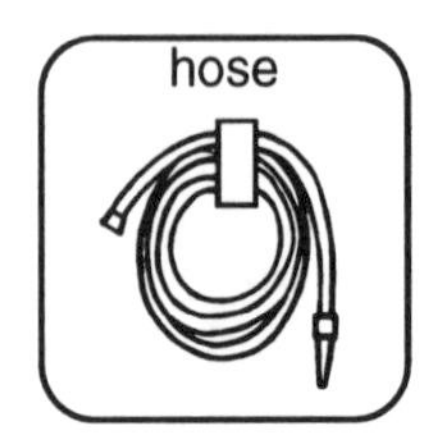

Police/Fire Station Follow-up Activity

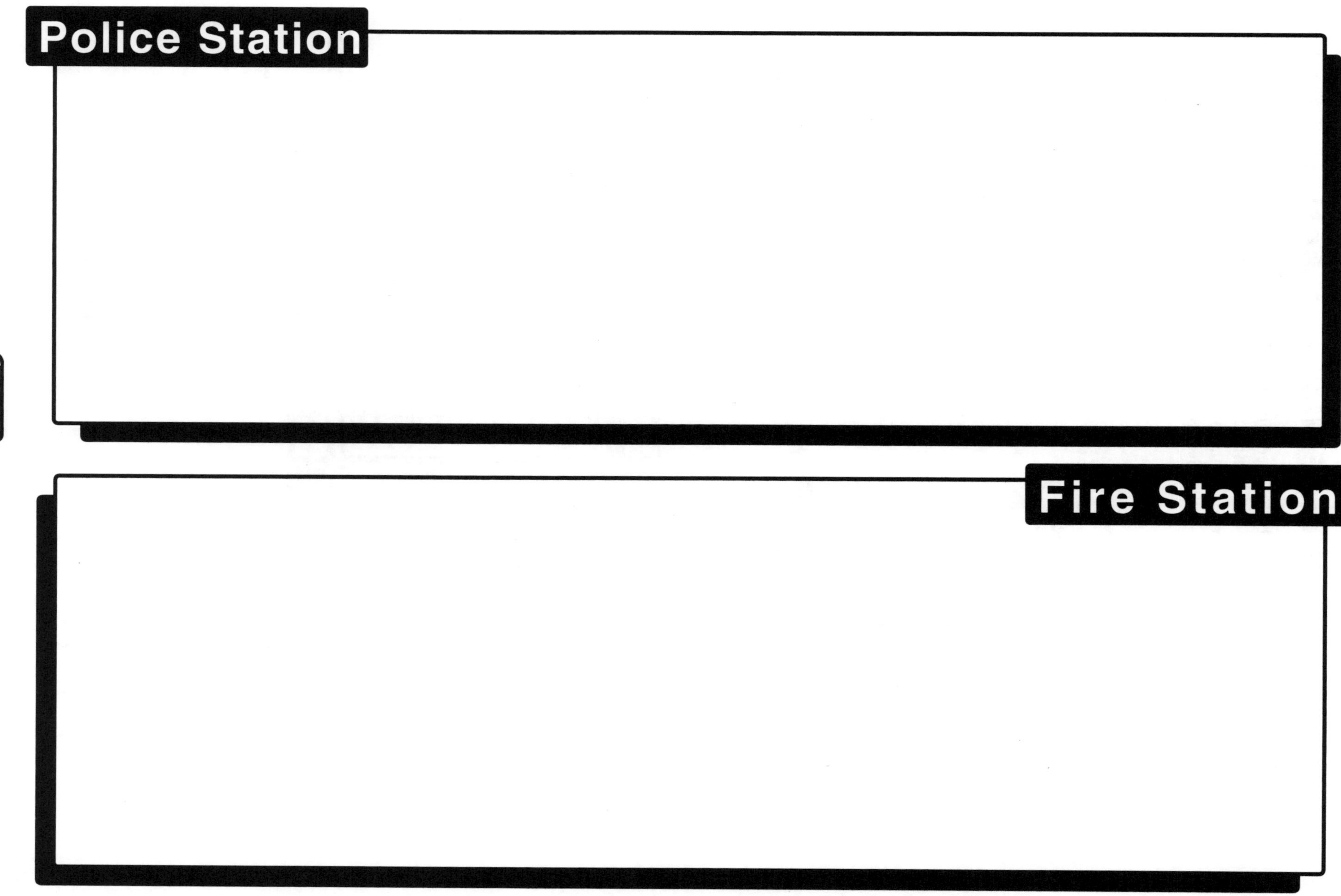

Police/Fire Station Follow-up Activity Cutouts

Directions: The following items are to be used with the Police/Fire Station Follow-up Activity, page 153. Duplicate both pages. Color, Cut out, and laminate items on this page. Attach a reusable adhesive (such as Fun-Tak®) to the back of each item. In addition, color, and laminate the Police/Fire Station Follow-up page. As you say the name of the item, have the student place it in either the police or fire station.

Police/Fire Station Charting Form Name ______________________

DATE				
Big				
Little				
Wet				
Dry				
Up				
Fire truck				
Police car				
Firefighter				
Police officer				
Siren				
Ladder				
Smoke detector				
Open				
Close				
Push				
Pull				
Yes				
No				
Please				
Thank you				

FINE MOTOR				
Opening door				
Closing door				
Cutting				
Coloring				
Change battery				
Using keys				
Painting				
Seat belts				
Tape recorder				

VP = Verbal Prompt PP = Physical Prompt HH = Hand Over Hand + = Independent - = Incapable

Notes:

Police/Fire Station
Related Materials

Books

Curious George Goes to the Police Station by Marget and H.A. Rey Adapted from the Curious George Film Series. ME:Houghton Mifflin Co., 1987.
Richard Scarry's Smokey and the Fireman by Richard Scarry. WI:Western Publishing Co., 1988.
Fireman Jim by Roger Bester. NY:Crown Publishers, Inc., 1981.
I Want to be a Policeman by Carla Greene. IL:Children's Press, 1958.
The Fire Station Book by Nancy Bundt. Ontario:J.M. Dent & Sons, 1981.
A Visit to the Sesame Street Firehouse by Dan Elliott. NY:Random House, Inc., 1983.

Related Software

Community Exploration available through Edmark
Signs Around You by Edmark
Community Activities available through Edmark
Looking for Words: Community available through Educational Resources

Related Toys

Dress-up clothing
Toy handcuffs
Toy fire truck
Toy police car